Contents

Contributors

Paula Lavis, former Information Specialist with the Royal College of Nursing, London, now with YoungMinds, London

Lesley Overall, Information Specialist, Quality Improvement Programme, Royal College of Nursing, London

Mapping Health on the Internet

Strategies for learning in an information age

Ross Scrivener

Information Manager
Quality Improvement Programme
Royal College of Nursing Institute
London

Radcliffe Medical Press

Radcliffe Medical Press Ltd
18 Marcham Road
Abingdon
Oxon OX14 1AA
United Kingdom

www.radcliffe-oxford.com
The Radcliffe Medical Press electronic catalogue and online ordering facility.
Direct sales to anywhere in the world.

© 2002 Ross Scrivener

British Library Cataloguing in Publication Data

A catalogue record for this book is available from the British Library.

ISBN 1 85775 593 6

Typeset by Advance Typesetting Ltd, Oxon
Printed and bound by TJ International Ltd, Padstow, Cornwall

My daughter Katy (aged nine) wanted to help me with this book, so she wrote the following dedication: 'For my precious daughters Emily and Katy and for my son Jamie. Also for my wife who has given support through writing this book.'

How to use this book

The idea for this book arose from my current job running a nursing information service with a particular focus on clinical effectiveness and quality improvement issues. The enquiries that we receive highlight the need for a publication that covers the diversity and value of material available on the Internet. This information is vital for healthcare professionals who are striving to keep their practice current and based on the best available evidence. The Internet will soon be the only sensible way of accessing publications such as clinical guidelines or systematic reviews, and of keeping up to date with key aspects of health service policy.

Chapter 1 addresses the problems associated with the Information Age. We need to understand the nature of the Internet before we can utilise it for our own purposes. The key to information literacy is twofold, namely gaining a better understanding of the information landscape, and being able to ask questions that focus investigations so that we gather only the specific information that we require.

Chapter 2 looks at how to ask questions that will make the information seeking more efficient and less frustrating. The question is the root that binds the bifurcating paths of the investigation together and anchors the research project. Time spent online incurs a cost. Planning a pathway from the question to key information sources reduces the risk of fruitless journeys.

Chapter 3 looks at how we can improve our understanding of the information landscape by using maps. We look at three different types of map, namely 'smart maps', concept maps and mind maps. These are all visual representations of subject areas that are designed to help users to grasp the range and relevance of sources of information.

We use mind maps to survey the information landscape in several clinical areas, including care of older people (Chapter 4), mental health (Chapter 5), child health (Chapter 6) and primary care (Chapter 7). A mind map precedes each chapter and provides an overview of the areas covered and a selection of the sites described within it.

In order to keep this book to a manageable length, we have used some criteria for including and excluding sites in the chapters that deal with specific clinical areas. The sites tend to originate from the UK. We wanted to explore those issues that dominate the lives of healthcare workers in the four countries of the UK. We have tended to exclude sites that require payment of some form of subscription; this means that we have omitted *e*-journals relating to the clinical topic areas. We hope that we have covered sites which, due to their provenance (governmental or academic), or their critical acceptance within the health service community, provide the best foundation for information research.

One of the key messages of this book is that we all need to sharpen our critical faculties when dealing with information on health issues. By the time you read this there will have been changes in the information landscape unforeseen by the author and his colleagues who helped to compile the chapters. This is the nature of the Internet (*see* Chapter 1).

Finally, Chapter 8 deals with the dynamic nature of the information landscape and the not too distant future.

Ross Scrivener
May 2002

1

Benefits and burdens of the Information Age

Information overload

Computers have infiltrated just about every aspect of information provision. Vast amounts of data can be processed at speeds that were unimaginable a few years ago. All kinds of data are available within a few clicks or keystrokes, and material can be retrieved, stored, manipulated and shared with increasing ease.

However, the information explosion has come at a price. Around 1000 books are published internationally every day, and the total amount of printed matter doubles every five years. More information has been produced in the last 30 years than in the previous 5000 years.[1]

New technologies have increased the pressure on organisations to promote communication internally as well as externally, intensifying the pressure on work forces. Dial-up information services have accelerated this trend. In 1985, 15 billion minutes were spent worldwide on the phone, talking, faxing and sending data. By 1995, this figure had quadrupled to 60 billion minutes, and it is now in excess of 95 billion minutes.[1]

Not surprisingly, people are finding it difficult to cope. In the UK alone, information overload contributes to up to 30 million working days lost through stress-related illnesses, at a cost of around two billion pounds.[1]

It has even been argued that the Information Age is a misnomer.[2] We live in an age that is struggling against the terrible onslaught of non-information. The science-fiction writer, Philip K Dick, coined the term 'kipple' for the worthless things threatening to engulf the universe. In *Do Androids Dream of Electric Sheep?*, 'kipple' poses a far greater threat to mankind than the super-intelligent, homicidal androids which are pursued through the novel.[3]

Familiarity with the signs and symptoms of information overload will help.

Types of information overload

Wilson and Walsh[4] have identified two forms of information overload, namely upkeep overload and task overload. Upkeep overload is the type of overload that is involved in maintaining the currency of our own knowledge base. For the busy clinician, keeping up to date with developments is a Herculean task. In 1993, Haynes[5] estimated that a doctor interested in adult internal medicine would need to read 17 articles a day for 365 days of the year in order to keep abreast of the literature.

Task overload is associated with the pursuit of information to meet a particular enquiry. Clinicians who are attempting to base their practice on the best available evidence are more likely to experience task overload unless they are given basic training in information seeking and knowledge management.

Signs and symptoms of information overload

The effects of information overload are insidious. Listed below are some of the ways in which it affects our decision making.

Mistaking data for knowledge

Data are often naively mistaken for knowledge, and we need to distinguish one from the other. Data are symbolic representations of real-world facts. They are raw, unrefined and not invested with meaning. Information consists of data put to work and into context. Data need to be reorganised and reordered before they can lead to insight and understanding. Knowledge is systematically connected information.

Stockpiling

Confronted by access to huge quantities of data, it is not surprising that people take the view that stockpiling is the only way to accumulate value and meaning. Data collection becomes an end in itself, and it becomes more difficult to separate the useful from the useless.

Failure to appraise information and time mismanagement

The exponential growth in our ability to store, retrieve and communicate information has outpaced our ability to keep track of it all. Decision makers have less time to evaluate and filter out irrelevant information, leading managers in commercial companies to wonder whether data collection has become a distraction from their main job responsibilities.[6]

Use of short cuts

Decision makers may apply another strategy to cope with the burden of information. They may devise short cuts[7] or simplistic rules of thumb to track down information. However, this information seeking may be based on nothing more discriminating than the visibility of or ease of access to a particular journal, author or institution.

All of these factors threaten our ability to make unbiased decisions.

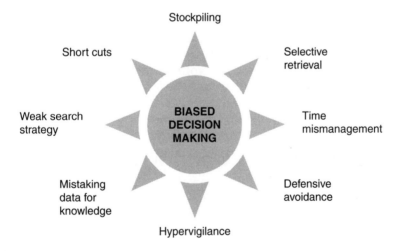

Figure 1.1 Information-seeking behaviour associated with information overload.

Box 1.1 How information overload threatens decision making

Theoretical models of stress shed light on how defective decision-making patterns develop. Vigilance is designated the optimum pattern, when all alternatives to a decision are analysed and interpreted in an unbiased fashion. However, experience, responsibility, uncertainty and conflict can all conspire to disrupt this process. This leads to two ineffective mechanisms for coping, namely defensive avoidance and hypervigilance.[4]

Defensive avoidance is the decision maker's attempt to avoid or postpone the stress of making the decision. It is manifested by procrastination and shifting of responsibility. Certain callers to our Information Service exhibit defensive avoidance. They confess that the reason for calling is that they need to give a presentation on the subject of clinical governance at an interview within 48 hours!

Hypervigilance represents a desperate search for a solution and a flight between alternatives. The decision maker seizes upon a possible solution impulsively, giving little thought to its shortcomings. As various forms of published 'evidence' proliferate, decision makers will be under increased pressure to implement findings. 'Quick-fix' solutions may result.

Two of the mediating conditions for optimum decision making are confidence that a better solution can be found, and time to search and deliberate. However, the sheer volume of information available increases the likelihood of defensive avoidance and hypervigilance.

The Internet and the World Wide Web

The Internet is bringing a cornucopia of resources to our desktops. However, it is simultaneously threatening to unleash an epidemic of information overload. If we are to find coping strategies and use the Internet effectively, we must be able to understand its basic mechanisms. It has three key characteristics, namely size, mutability and interconnectedness.

The Internet is the linkage of a large number of computers around the world, ranging from personal computers to supercomputers, into one huge network that in effect provides a vast database of information for anyone connected to it. The World Wide Web is the collection of websites on the Internet.

How big is the Web? The fact is that we do not know exactly. Part of the problem is that Web content can mean individual pages, sites or objects, such as video and images. One estimate puts the number of objects on the indexable Web as around 320 million, but it could have been as high as 800 million for 1998.[8]

The challenge now is to capture the richness of the Web by cataloguing and indexing it in the same way that traditional libraries do. This is made difficult because the Web is like a living organism (*see* Box 1.2). Web objects have life cycles. They can disappear and reappear. They can disappear forever, or the Web address may still exist but point to non-existent content. All these patterns of behaviour pose serious problems for the integrity and usefulness of libraries and information services that are attempting to create collections of Web content.

A third feature of the Web, and by some way the most important, is its interconnectedness. This is due to the use of links, known as hypertext links, which can provide the means to navigate both within a site and to other related sites. Hypertext links are like a signpost pointing one way. They take you directly to the destination on the sign.

Box 1.2 The librarian's nightmare – how to manage the Web?

Like all sources of information, the contents of the Web can be organised, collected and managed rather in the manner of traditional libraries. However, whereas traditional collections may deteriorate over time or even be subjected to active eradication, websites and web pages are more likely to be subject to content change and attrition.

Koehler's studies[8] provide some insight into the pace of this change. The half-life of a web page is somewhat less than two years, and the half-life of a website is somewhat more than two years. A web document collection created two years ago would contain the same number of URLs (web addresses), but only half of them would point to actual content. Nearly all web pages undergo some form of change within a year.

Publishers may bring out further editions of a book, but previous editions of the book will still remain. However, when a web document is edited or updated, the antecedent is eradicated. One of the many paradoxes of the World Wide Web is that the availability of Web content is continually at risk from the technology delivering it.

Imagine a library where the very existence of the collection is continually in question. Librarians who manage Web resources are just beginning to understand the impact of Web document metamorphoses and develop methods to safeguard their collections.

My 10-year-old daughter's class has been researching the Tudors. By the time my 4-year-old son gets to do the same project, it is likely to be (in part at least) a Web-based exercise. If properly guided, the child could quickly find recommended history sites and search for primary sources such as an online version of Ann Boleyn's speech at her execution, descriptions of how food was preserved, and sound archives of Tudor music.

The Internet is a maze

This sounds wonderful in theory. I can go to a site of interest and explore other related sites listed by it. The downside is that without careful planning and management we can very easily become lost and confused.

In a very real sense the Web exhibits the characteristics of a maze. Every maze has an entrance and must have one goal – a point in the maze that you try to find. To solve the maze you must find a route from the entrance to the goal. There may be more than one route, but the implicit puzzle involves finding the shortest route.

The difficulty of tackling a maze is bound up with the number of branches it has from each forking path. Think of this in relation to a website. A website contains links both to other parts of the site and to other sites of interest. It is very tempting to try to explore these and then quickly lose sight of the goal – the reason why you entered the maze in the first place.

Inside a maze it is easy to become disorientated. Maze designers consciously use features such as hedges and walls to make each path look the same. You feel as if you are going round in circles when in fact you are not.

The structure of websites induces a similar sense of disorientation. For instance, we have pointed out that hyperlinks are unidirectional but they may lead you to four different types of destination, namely a location within the same document, a document on the same website, a document on another website and a program that results in a web page.

We can also arrive at a page by a number of different means – a link from within the site, a link from outside the site or a link created from a text search. Because there is an absence of physical context within a website, the reader can only see one page at a time. Therefore website designers need to ensure that the reader's idea of what the website contains is presented and reinforced on each page.

Sadly, website design is still in its infancy, and fundamental errors of design are reproduced and perpetuated by prominent websites. Whereas fortunes have been invested in traditional text retrieval systems and library catalogues, and whole institutions exist to help us to fulfil our information needs, parallel developments online remain fairly crude.

Figure 1.2 The simplest type of maze.[9] This is an example of a unicursal maze. It is the simplest form of maze. The paths do not fork, and you can only go in one direction until you reach the goal. Unfortunately, the Web behaves like a maze with multiple branching paths. It is more complex than any maze ever built.

Information quality

Information is the commodity of the Web. One of the realities of dot.com economics is that the main cost of creating and selling information occurs at the time of production. However, because web pages can be put together so cheaply and quickly, producers with low production costs can flood the marketplace with poor-quality information.

This is particularly damaging for healthcare. Large sums of money may be spent on labour-intensive projects such as clinical guidelines in an effort to disseminate the best evidence, only for the amount of biased, outdated or inaccurate information to have grown exponentially in the mean time. Varian[10] puts a fresh spin on Malthus' law. Malthus stated that the number of human stomachs grows geometrically but the amount of food grows linearly. Similarly, the amount of information or 'kipple' inflates alarmingly, but the amount that is consumed grows at best linearly. To put this another way, the fraction of information that is consumed as a proportion of the overall amount of information which is produced plunges towards zero.

Box 1.3 Memes: how ideas like viruses replicate and spread on the Internet

Professor Richard Dawkins, in his book *The Selfish Gene*,[11] coined the term 'memes' to describe the self-replicating patterns of information that behave like viruses. They are copied from person to person, gaining authority with each new host. Examples of memes in the animal world include birdsongs and hunting techniques. In human society almost any cultural entity can be regarded as a meme. Memes may be silly and foolish like 'urban myths', or they may involve religious beliefs, political ideas or scientific theories, conventions and concepts.

The structure of the Internet and its very interconnectedness makes the rapid spread of memes inevitable. Discussion groups, bulletin boards and virtual newsletters provide a fertile breeding ground for them. Dawkins itemised three characteristics for any successful replicator, namely *copying fidelity* (the more faithful the copy, the more will remain of the original pattern), *fecundity* (the replicator spreads according to the rate of copying) and *longevity* (the longer the replicator survives, the greater the number of copies that can be made of it). The global network greatly increases the efficiency of replication. Digitisation allows a much higher degree of copying fidelity than any analogue method. Computer networks accelerate the rate of copying and, potentially at least, storage on disk or other archiving prolongs the life of the meme.

'Memetic bombardment'[12] is an intrinsic part of the Information Age. Will it lead us to prefer short, catchy memes to lengthy explanations? Is there a risk that the most fertile memes will have less long-term value and authority? Perhaps the most pernicious memes are those consumer health sites that offer incomplete and contradictory information.[13]

The implications for healthcare

Why should this affect healthcare professionals? If the Web is as chaotic as the statistics indicate, why bother with it in the first place? It is true that the Web can be daunting and frustrating, but the pace of change is intense and the stakes are high for governments and commerce alike.

Information provision within the National Health Service is undergoing a sea change. The *Information for Health* strategy[14] from the Department of Health marked a shift in policy. For the first time it was acknowledged that patients and clinicians, not managers, should be the first to harvest the benefits of a well-developed information infrastructure for the NHS.

Ambitious projects such as the National electronic Library for Health[15] and NHS Direct Online[16] (*see* Boxes 1.4 and 1.5) are the direct result of governmental aspirations. The aim of both sites is to provide users – whether they are health practitioners, patients or members of the public – with access to credible and reliable information.

Another strand of official policy is the emphasis on lifelong learning, both in terms of the development of individual health professionals and at the level of the wider service. Davies identifies three levels of learning.[17] The first level is basic correction of error – so-called 'single-loop' learning. Clinical audit is an example of this. Reconfiguring services to follow new strategic paths or redefining care delivery in the light of evidence-based practice requires a more radical approach to learning – the second level or so-called 'double-loop' learning. Successful learning organisations will be adept at promoting both. They will devote time and resources to using the experience of such projects, and by doing so they will demonstrate a third level of learning – meta-learning, or learning about learning. We shall revisit these themes in the final chapter.

Box 1.4 The National electronic Library for Health

The National electronic Library for Health[15] (NeLH) was first muted in the document *Information for Health*,[14] which was published at the end of 1998. The document marked a radical departure in strategic thinking about the use of information and information technology in the NHS. It proposes that investment in technology should benefit patients and clinicians rather than focus on financial and managerial imperatives. The creation of the NeLH is an attempt to harness Internet technologies to meet the needs of these groups wherever they may be in the UK.

The mission of the NeLH can be summarised quite simply. It is to provide easy access to best current knowledge and to improve health and healthcare, patient choice and clinical practice. It is founded on certain key principles that are worth stating here.

- It will concentrate on the quality rather than the quantity of evidence.
- It will contain 'know-how' (i.e. guidelines and audit) as well as knowledge.
- It will be available to patients and clinicians, managers and the public.
- It will only exist in electronic form.
- It will involve users in strategic decisions about its development.

It is helpful to imagine the virtual library as a building with 'floors'. On entering the library you will find an atrium with help desks and links to virtual branch libraries. Plans exist for numerous branch libraries, but you can visit two of the most advanced of these – for primary care (the NeLH-PC)[18] and for mental health (the NeLMH).[19]

There is a floor containing guidelines and audit information. The National Institute for Clinical Excellence will be a key provider for this area. Another floor will incorporate information from quality-assured studies and collated evidence such as systematic reviews. Information from studies will be available in different formats such as brief 'bottom lines' and more detailed summaries.

Patient information will be provided via access to NHS Direct Online.[16] Branch libraries will collaborate with NHS Direct Online and develop joint themed events. The knowledge management floor will concentrate on helping users to develop skills associated with informatics and evidence-based practice (e.g. searching bibliographic databases and critical appraisal skills).

The director of the NeLH, Dr Muir Gray, envisages another role for the NeLH and its branch libraries. The library will host 'cyber societies' where people, as well as facts, will be connected.[20] These discussion groups are another means of sharing 'knowledge' and obtaining insight.

Box 1.5 NHS Direct Online

NHS Direct Online[16] provides patients and the public with health information. NHS Direct is not solely Web based. It is a helpline staffed by nurses.

Its features include the following.

Health Features – a monthly 'magazine' devoted to a single topic of interest, such as travel health. These features will link with items in the relevant National electronic Library for Health virtual branch library. For instance, a 'Health Feature' on the subject of depression will link to the National electronic Library for Mental Health.

Healthcare Guide – a guide to aid the treatment of common symptoms at home.

Condition and Treatment – links to thousands of sources of help and advice. This includes several elements that exploit the electronic format. First, the user can access the clinical topic of choice by a number of means, one of which is an interactive body map. For instance, by clicking on the eyes the user can view a list of conditions, including blindness, conjunctivitis and glaucoma. If the user selects glaucoma at this point, the next screen will show support organisations, evaluated patient information and audio clips relating to that condition. The leaflets listed are quality checked by the Centre for Health Information Quality[21] using the DISCERN[22] instrument, and are given a star rating. Only those documents that rank as three stars or higher are included in the list. Many of these hyperlink to the host organisations where the patient information is displayed. The glaucoma page lists leaflets from the International Glaucoma Association[23] and Moorfields Eye Hospital.[24]

Listen here audio clips – users can listen to features recorded in a number of languages. This feature is used in the Conditions and Treatment section and appears in other sections of the site.

A–Z guide to the NHS – this feature includes information on how to get help from NHS services such as benefits, Social Services and residential care.

Other features include occasional features promoting 'Healthy Living', links to the NHS Direct phone lines, and information showing the extent of coverage of this service.

The challenge that this presents to the health service is enormous. Even the government talks in terms of a 'ten-year programme'. The diffusion of information via the Internet is one way in which individuals and health-care organisations can learn both about the effectiveness or otherwise of interventions and about the implementation of strategies known to change clinicians' behaviour.

An Information Age paradox

We are confronted by a fundamental Information Age paradox. We know that the information we require is out there somewhere in the heart of this maze we call the Web, but we do not have the luxury of time or an unlimited Internet account. We need to be familiar with the information landscape before we can utilise it, and if we explore it before we are familiar with it we are going to get hopelessly lost.

So what are the options?

Invest in search engines

Search engines are a means of searching for information on the Web. They use various strategies to locate information that matches the words used in your query. Search engines are being continually refined to improve their performance. They are quick, relatively straightforward to use, and good at retrieving information on popular subjects.

Unfortunately, each search engine has its own limitations and idiosyncrasies. Many of the most popular search engines search only a fraction of the indexable Web (*see* Chapter 2). They inevitably retrieve hundreds or thousands of pieces of 'information'. If we are lucky, some of these might suit our needs, but few people have the time to appraise them all. Clinicians who are thinking about using the Web to locate information would be better off searching specialised databases or gateways of evaluated sites (e.g. OMNI; *see* Chapter 2).

Invest in people

Another option is to invest in people and train individuals in the techniques required to undertake information research. Two priority areas are developing our strategies for searching and broadening our meta-knowledge – our knowledge of where things are.

Table 1.1 Changing search methods

	Weak searching paradigm	*Strong searching paradigm*
1 Relies on:	Popular search engines	Specialist meta-databases and gateways
2 Focuses on:	Single studies	Systematically collated evidence
3 Trusts in:	Serendipity	Information services and networks

It is vitally important that we exchange the weaker search paradigm for the stronger one identified in Table 1.1. Failure to do so will result in further indiscriminate and biased selections from an electronic morass. We need to abandon notions that the Web is a luxury, fad or distraction. The word 'surfing' must be excised from our vocabulary. Web 'searching' is always planned, purposeful and pertinent.

Chapter 2 explores in more depth the issues surrounding questions and searching, while Chapter 3 offers a strategy for improving orientation in relation to healthcare information.

Summary

Benefits of the Information Age:

- increasing computer memory
- increasing processing speed
- increasing accessibility of a range of different types of information.

Burdens of the Information Age:

- information inflation
- information overload
- as information increases, the fraction that is actually consumed decreases.

Information overload impairs decision making by leading us to:

- mistake data for knowledge
- gather excessive data
- use short cuts.

The Web is characterised by its growing size, mutability and inter-connectedness. It has yet to develop sophisticated systems for information retrieval, and online time is increasingly being threatened by the increase in poor-quality information.

The Web will play a crucial role in lifelong learning for health professionals, and NHS projects promise unprecedented access to information for patients and clinicians. However, we are caught in an Information Age paradox – you need to be familiar with the information landscape before you can exploit it properly, but if you explore it before you are familiar with it, you will get hopelessly lost.

Key competencies for health professionals will include search and information-mapping skills.

References

1 Reuters Business Information (1997) *Dying for Information. An investigation into the effects of information overload in the UK and worldwide*. Reuters Business Information, London.

2 Wurman RS (1989) *Information Anxiety*. Pan, London.

3 Dick PK (1968) *Do Androids Dream of Electric Sheep?* Del Rey, New York.

4 Wilson PT and Walsh C (1996) *Information Behaviour: an inter-disciplinary perspective. A Report to the British Library Research and Innovation Centre on a*

review of the literature. British Library Board; http://www.shef.ac.uk/uni/academic/I-M/is/publications/prelims.html

5 Haynes RB (1993) Where's the meat in clinical journals? *ACP Journals Club.* **119**: A23–4. Quoted by Davidoff F, Haynes B, Sackett D and Smith R (1995) Evidence-based medicine. *BMJ.* **310**: 1085–6.

6 Hall H (1997) *Networked Information: dealing with overload.* In: Proceedings of Information Scotland, Strathclyde Business School, 4 November 1997. Library Association, Cataloguing and Indexing Group Scotland, Paisley; http://imdept.qmuc.ac.uk/imres/fulltxt/txt_HH4.htm

7 Biggs M (1989) Information overload and information seekers: what we know about them, what we do about them. *Ref Librarian.* **25**: 411–29. Quoted in Parker S (1999) The implementation of intranet technology as a solution to information overload in the top 100 commercial organisations in the UK; http://www.geocities.com/Tokyo/Subway/7854/ack.htm

8 Koehler W (1999) Digital libraries and the World Wide Web sites and page persistence. School of Library and Information Studies, University of Oklahoma; http://www.shef.ac.uk/~is/publications/infres/paper60.html

9 http://www.gwydir.demon.co.uk/jo/maze/

10 Varian HR (1998) *Markets for Information Goods.* University of California, Berkeley, CA; http://www.sims.berkeley.edu/~hal/Papers/japan/

11 Dawkins R (1976) *The Selfish Gene.* Oxford University Press, Oxford.

12 Blackmore S (1999) *The Meme Machine.* Oxford University Press, Oxford.

13 California Health Care Foundation (2001) *Proceed with Caution. A report on the quality of health information on the Internet.* California Health Care Foundation, Oakland, CA; http://www.chcf.org

14 NHS Executive (1998) *Information for Health: an information strategy for the modern NHS 1998–2005.* NHS Executive, Leeds.

15 http://www.nelh.nhs.uk/

16 http://www.nhsdirect.nhs.uk/

17 Davies HT and Nutley SM (2000) Developing learning organisations in the new NHS. *BMJ.* **320**: 998–1001.

18 http://www.nelh-pc.nhs.uk/

19 http://www.nelmh.org/

20 Muir Gray JA and de Lusignan S (1999) National electronic Library for Health (NeLH). *BMJ.* **319**: 1476–9.

21 http://www.hfht.org/chiq/

22 http://www.discern.org.uk/

23 http://www.iga.org.uk/

24 http://www.moorfields.org.uk/ef-glaucoma.html

Questioning and searching

What is information literacy?

It seems that once upon a time, long ago, the key educational competencies were numeracy, reading and writing. Our jobs had tangible outputs that could be weighed and measured. This is no longer the case. The familiar competencies are no longer adequate. Our workplaces are changing and we are being challenged to adapt to new working environments.

Information literacy[1] can be summarised as the ability to:

- recognise a need for information
- identify and locate information sources
- know how to gain access to the information contained in those sources
- evaluate the quality of information obtained
- organise the information
- use the information effectively.

The document *Learning to Manage Health Information*[2] sets out key 'expectations for learning' for health professionals. These include the following:

- locating specified online health-related information and identifying 'trusted'/validated sources of data and information relevant to the health domain
- developing a specific query in response to a problem and search for answers
- using and critically appraising evidence to support patient care.

The first expectation is the subject of Chapter 3. This is the concept of mapping and maintaining a current knowledge of information sources. The focus of the present chapter will be the issues contained within the second point – that is, how we identify the components of a clinical question.

Questioning

The reflective practitioner will need to adopt methods that will take him or her beyond traditional teaching systems designed fundamentally to impart meanings for students. The consequence of the move towards a competency-based approach to learning is an additional burden on students. Every learner is required to be a 'self-starter' and to have acquired basic learning skills. At the top of this list of skills is the ability to ask questions.

Questions are probably the most powerful information technology known to man. However, the ability to ask questions is a skill that is traditionally neglected in the school setting.[3] The nature of the Internet demands that users spend more time thinking about their information needs and develop their own 'information literacy'. We need to find ways to convert our information needs into focused questions.

Focusing and refocusing questions

When people begin to assess their information needs they tend to ask very broad questions. The following are examples of questions that have been received by our information service.

- Could you send me everything you have on clinical audit methods?
- How do I start writing protocols for running clinics?

Many callers ask similar questions about generic issues. Our response is to get them to relate the enquiry back to their context and the trigger for the enquiry. For instance, it is much easier to get to grips with the notion of clinical guidelines if we know that the caller is a practice nurse who intends to update diabetic clinic protocols.

Here is a further selection of questions pulled from our enquiries database.

- Is gentamicin cover necessary when replacing or taking out catheters?
- What do studies of patient satisfaction with breast care services indicate for clinicians?
- What guidance exists about securing endotracheal tubes in children?
- Are there clinical pathways for the management of spinal injury?
- Have protocols been developed for the management of anaphylactic reactions?

- Are there audit tools for perioperative pain management?
- Is there published evidence from randomised controlled trials about the efficacy of care pathways?
- What is best practice in asthma management in a school setting?

Although these questions cover a wide variety of subjects, they have certain features in common. They are all rooted in real-world problems. They are more focused questions than the first set of questions. They are using efficient methods for finding the information required. Recognising the key elements of good questions will help us to track down relevant information (*see* Box 2.1).

Box 2.1 What are the key components of a good clinical question?

There is a growing literature on what constitutes a good clinical question.[4-6] Typically these texts concentrate on teasing out the following key components.

Step 1: Start by defining the *patient* or *problem*. Who is the focus of the question? Think of the characteristics of this group.

Step 2: Now what is the *intervention* under consideration? This could be a drug treatment or an operation. However, the question might not necessarily be concerned with an intervention as such. It might be a question about *exposure* – assessing the potential risk to a patient travelling overseas of contracting particular illnesses.

Step 3: What is the *outcome*? This could be framed to be desirable (e.g. the reduced risk of having a heart attack after being put on a certain diet, better quality of life following the intervention) or undesirable (e.g. the risk of an adverse reaction after taking a particular drug).

The elements can best be remembered using the PICO mnemonic – **p** for patient or problem, **i** for intervention, **c** for comparison intervention, where necessary, and **o** for outcome.

Imagining the journey from problem to action

Let us put our search for clinical evidence into context. The search is one part of a process – a journey from identifying a real-world problem to making a decision about whether to change current practice and following up the consequences of that decision. The whole process can be represented as a flow chart (*see* Figure 2.1).

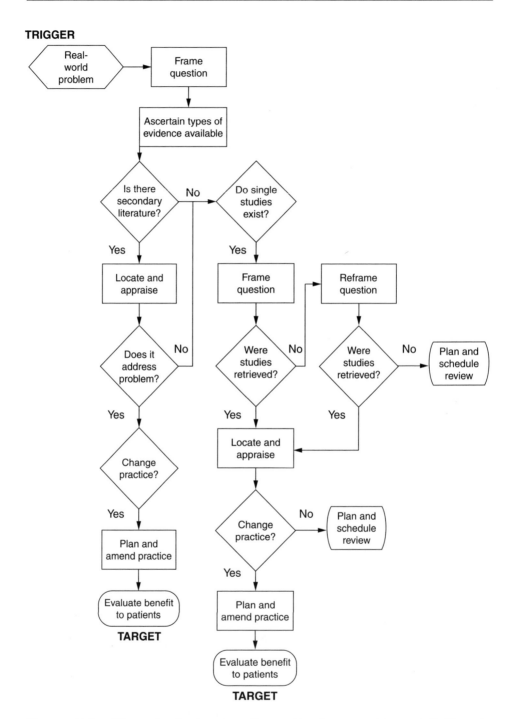

Figure 2.1 Flow chart showing the route from problem definition to changing practice.

Strengths and weaknesses of evidence

Any search for information begins with the identification of a clinical question and then a search to ascertain how much research evidence is available that addresses it. In the light of this 'mapping' of the evidence you might narrow or broaden the focus of the original question.

Recognising that the literature reports on various levels of evidence will help you to retrieve the most appropriate evidence for a particular clinical question (*see* Box 2.2). Remember that the 'best' evidence will be the evidence that is most relevant to answering the question. This depends on the type and amount of research evidence available and what is feasible given the time and resources that you have available.

Box 2.2 What do we mean by primary and secondary literature?

Studies that present the results of original research are referred to as *primary literature.*

Secondary literature refers to a heterogeneous group of publications which all use strategies to collate or synthesise published studies on a particular topic. Their aim is to direct clinical decision making based on the best available evidence.

Evidence-based clinical practice guidelines – 'systematically developed statements to assist the practitioner and patient decisions about appropriate healthcare for specific circumstances'.[7]

Systematic reviews – use explicit and rigorous methods to identify, critically appraise and synthesise relevant studies in answer to articulated questions. They appraise relevant published and unpublished evidence before combining and analysing data. They form the basis of evidence-based clinical practice guidelines. A key resource for finding systematic reviews is the Cochrane Library.[8]

Critically appraised topics (CATs) – provide commentary on the strength of a study and its clinical significance. They can be found in journals such as *Clinical Evidence,*[9] *Evidence-Based Medicine*[10] and *ACP Journal Club,*[11] but are increasingly evident online in the form of 'CAT banks' (e.g. there is one at the Centre for Evidence-Based Medicine.[12]

Health technology assessments (HTAs) – the HTA[13] programme is a national programme of research established and funded by the Department of Health's Research and Development programme. The purpose of the programme is to ensure that high-quality research information on the costs, effectiveness and broader impact of health technologies is produced in the most effective way for those who use, manage and provide care in the NHS. 'Technologies' in this context are not confined to new drugs or pieces of sophisticated equipment. They cover any method used by those working in the health services to promote health, prevent and treat disease and improve rehabilitation and long-term care. The National Institute for Clinical Excellence[14] also commissions work as part of this programme, and the Health Technology Board for Scotland[15] performs the equivalent function for NHS Scotland.

National Service Frameworks (NSFs) – define explicit standards and principles for the pattern and level of services required. National Service Frameworks[16] set national standards and define service models for a specific service or care group, put in place programmes to support implementation, and establish performance measures against which progress within an agreed timescale will be measured. Building on the frameworks for cancer and paediatric intensive care, the first two NSFs are for mental health[17] (published in September 1999) and coronary heart disease[18] (published in March 2000). NSFs have been developed for older people,[19] and diabetes.[20] Plans for NSFs for children[21] and long-term conditions[22] are well developed. There will usually be only one new topic each year.

Information from 'secondary' publications derived from evidence-based literature (e.g. clinical guidelines, systematic reviews or critically appraised topics) has the potential to bring the greatest amount of research evidence to bear on a question with the least amount of time and effort on your part.

You should be aware that even findings from these publications should be critically appraised for credibility and applicability to your clinical setting.

It is quite likely that you will not find a secondary publication that addresses your problem, for all kinds of reasons. In this case you should try to locate and appraise studies from all potentially relevant studies that appear in primary publications (i.e. publications of original research appearing in peer-reviewed journals). This may take considerable time and effort if a large number of studies are involved.

Getting organised

You need to be realistic about what you can achieve. First, you must not assume that you will have all of the skills for all of the stages of this process from the outset. These will be acquired incrementally over time. Secondly, by using a set of reliable resources such as those listed in Table 2.1 you can find information more efficiently, saving yourself time and effort. Thirdly, if possible you should involve others in the project and look for support either inside or outside your workplace. There may be research or other clinical improvement networks into which you can tap.

Table 2.1 Table of clinical evidence resources

Type of evidence	Source	Online availability
Simultaneous search of secondary and primary literature	SUMSearch	http://sumsearch.uthscsa.edu/
Secondary literature National clinical guidelines	National Institute for Clinical Excellence	http://www.nice.org.uk/
	National Guideline Clearing House (USA)	http://www.guidelines.gov/
	National electronic Library for Health	http://www.nelh.nhs.uk/
	Scottish Intercollegiate Guideline Network Professional bodies (i.e. medical colleges, etc.)	http://www.sign.ac.uk/
Systematic reviews	Cochrane Library	http://www.update-software.com/clibhome/clib.htm
	Centre for Reviews and Dissemination (University of York)	http://www.york.ac.uk/inst/crd/
	Health Evidence Bulletins (Wales)	http://www.uwcm.ac.uk/uwcm/lb/pep
National Service Frameworks	Department of Health	http://www.doh.gov.uk/nsf/nsfhome.htm
Health technology assessments	National Institute for Clinical Excellence (England and Wales)	http://www.nice.org.uk
	Health Technology Board for Scotland (Scotland)	http://www.htbs.org.uk/
Critically appraised topics (CATs)	CAT banks	http://cebm.jr2.ox.ac.uk/docs.catbank.html
	Clinical Evidence from *BMJ*	http://www.clinicalevidence.org
Standards or consensus statements	Professional bodies (e.g. Royal College of Nursing) Government departments	http://www.rcn.org.uk/

Table 2.1 Continued

Type of evidence	Source	Online availability
Primary literature Research papers (quantitative or qualitative)	Bibliographic databases – online (e.g. MEDLINE is available online as PubMed), British Nursing Index or CINAHL (subscription service only, or free from Royal College of Nursing library) Other online journals (e.g. *BMJ* online)	http://www.ncbi.nlm.nih.gov/ PubMed/
Ongoing research	National Research Register	http://www.update-software.com/ nrronline/
Tacit knowledge	Discussion lists (e.g. Mailbase lists, CHAIN)	http://www.jiscmail.ac.uk/ http://www.open.gov.uk/doh/ ntrd/chain/chain.html
Gateways	Specific Internet gateways (e.g. PEDINFO for paediatric sites) Health gateways (e.g. OMNI, NMAP)	http://www.pedinfo.org/ http://omni.ac.uk http://nmap.ac.uk/
Internet search sites	Altavista, Yahoo, Google, etc.	http://www.altavista.com http://www.google.com

Remember that failure to engage in research-based practice will result in care that is out of date. Investing in this process can lead to tangible benefits for your patients and professional satisfaction in the longer term.

Rules of thumb when searching: fast and frugal heuristics

We all use rules of thumb or 'heuristics' to make decisions in our daily lives. Research into the use of heuristics by clinicians has tended to emphasise situations where their use is problematic.[23,24] However, recent studies[25] have explored the extent to which we routinely rely on heuristics to make inferences about the world. Practitioners must develop their own robust and discriminating heuristics for searching information. These rules of thumb need to be 'fast and frugal' – fast in relation to their computation time, and frugal in the sense that they must be efficient.

Ascertaining the type of evidence available

Just how fast and efficient our search is going to be is critically dependent on our familiarity with the knowledge base and where to find things. We do not want to be spending too long trawling through sources where there is little or no likelihood of retrieving information to meet our needs.

Each clinician, regardless of their specialty, can construct a table similar to the one shown in Table 2.1, showing the most useful and appropriate online resources for their field. This table could act as a series of prompts or cues for tracking evidence. It could also act as an *aide-mémoire* for resources that are not available on the Web. Part of the problem with assembling such a table is the multiplicity of resources available. The plurality of the Web is both a help and a hindrance. Where does one begin?

Evaluating the quality of information on the Internet

The table represents the types of sites that are available for answering a clinical query. The best place to start with this kind of query is to find out whether any secondary literature addresses the problem. Table 2.1 covers some sources of secondary literature.

Another resource which should be near the top of the table is one dedicated to your particular specialty or subject area. These are often referred to as *gateways* or *portals*. They will be useful for two reasons. First, the inclusion criteria tend to be explicit, so you know what you are likely to get. Secondly, they are usually searchable or offer a classification structure which is easily navigable. Both of these features should reduce the risk of irrelevant items and wasted effort. If you are affiliated to a particular professional body, that organisation's website will often act as a gateway or 'reputation manager' for credible links and resources.

People are a valuable online resource

Remember that the Internet networks people as well, so *tacit knowledge* must feature in the table. You can access expertise by researching news-groups and discussion lists.

Do not assume that you will find it on the Web

We must bear in mind that although the number of quality information sources is growing, the resources available in libraries will complement and augment the search. However, a well-conceived online search should identify items for follow-up outside the Web itself, and will help to locate these items.

Searching different types of resources

Our ladder of resources has identified evidence by type – secondary literature, primary literature and tacit knowledge. This information is made available by a variety of different means, including databases, online documents and articles, discussion groups and search engines.

In order to take full advantage of the range of evidence and expertise available, we need to become proficient in the use of all of these methods. Boxes 2.3, 2.4, 2.5 and 2.6 take examples of a database, an online publication, a discussion group and two gateways to highlight how electronic media are expanding search options.

Box 2.3 Searching an online bibliographic database: the case of PubMed

PubMed is the National Library of Medicine platform for searching MEDLINE.[26] MEDLINE is one of the premier sources of bibliographic and abstract coverage of biomedical literature, and it indexes around 3800 journals. Although it includes a nursing index, the British Nursing Index[27] and CINAHL[28] are more comprehensive sources for nursing subject matter. MEDLINE contains about 11 million records.

Medical Subject Headings (MeSH) – like many bibliographic databases, MEDLINE includes a thesaurus of terms which can be used to run both simple and advanced queries. MeSH terms are used to describe the abstract of each journal incorporated within the database. Reviewers typically assign around 10 or 12 MeSH terms to each article, and you can choose to view these by clicking on the 'citations' button.

MeSH contains about 19 000 terms which are updated annually to keep abreast of changes in medicine and medical terminology. MeSH is hierarchical – it groups headings under subject categories and puts broader terms above more specific ones. This means that you can select a MeSH term and use it to add precision to your search.

Other features

Other Search Fields – you can hone your search by incorporating other search fields, such as Author Name and Publication Date. You can also search on Publication Type – for example, Clinical Trial (which includes all randomised controlled trials) and Review (which includes systematic reviews).

Clinical Queries – this automatically filters searches on questions of therapy, diagnosis, aetiology or prognosis by looking for the highest levels of evidence in the literature.

LinkOut – certain abstracts within PubMed link to full-text journal articles. The host sites of these articles sometimes require user registration or some other type of fee in order to view the article. Others, such as those linked to the eBMJ[29] site, do not.

See Related Articles – this function will retrieve additional articles based on an algorithm of key words and Medical Subject Headings (MeSH headings).

Box 2.4 Searching an online journal: the case of the eBMJ

The eBMJ[29] is a good example of what can be achieved using the available technologies. Instead of replicating the traditional format of the medical journal, a great deal of effort has gone into exploiting the functionality of the Web for the user's benefit. The functions listed below are currently available at no cost to the user.

Search/Archive – the eBMJ incorporates every issue of the *BMJ* that has appeared since January 1994. You can search for articles using a template. Search fields include author name(s) and words appearing either in the abstract or anywhere in the article. The results of the search can be viewed either as an abstract or as full text. You can also choose to search other participating journals.

Collections – eBMJ organises articles and other items into collections, which range from clinical topics to subjects such as quality improvement and medical informatics.

Inter-journal links – articles cited by features and which are published by HighWire Press[30] (a free full-text science archive run by Stamford University) are available to the user by the use of hyperlinks. By clicking on the hyperlink, you can view the abstract identified by the citation in the original eBMJ.

Online debates, discussions and questionnaires – eBMJ posts the results of debates on its website. One poll asking whether doctors and nurses should monitor each other's performance received over 2000 replies.

CiteTrack – you can tell the eBMJ site to alert you via email if it or a participating journal publishes new content matching criteria set by you.

Box 2.5 Searching for tacit knowledge: the case of JISCmail

JISCmail[31] supports electronic discussion lists for the UK higher education community. The topics listed under the 'Medicine and Health' category include aspects of evidence-based practice such as critical appraisal skills and a list dedicated to issues surrounding the development of systematic reviews.

What is a discussion group?
A discussion group is a group of people with a common interest. List members can talk with other list members via email. JISCmail makes joining the list a simple procedure. Once you have registered with a list or lists you can send a message to the list and that message will be sent to all of the members on the list.

You can search for lists that match your interests or browse alphabetically to view the range of subjects covered by the lists. For instance, the DIST-NURSE list is described as a 'UK-based list to bring together ideas and views from the wide community of district nurses. The list will encourage sharing of research findings, relevant conferences and the impact of policy on the role of the district nurse. Research and educational opportunities are fundamental to the practice of district nursing. The list will be of great value to practitioners and educationalists'.

Box 2.6 Searching a gateway: the case of OMNI and NMAP

OMNI[32] (Organising Medically Networked Information) and NMAP[33] (Nursing, Midwifery and Allied Health Professionals) are gateways to evaluated resources on the Internet. The University of Nottingham hosts both gateways.

OMNI covers medicine, biomedicine, allied health, health management and related topics. NMAP covers topics from the perspective of nursing, midwifery and allied health professionals.

Evaluation criteria – each of the records held by the gateways has been subject to an evaluation process. These cover questions that assess the following:

• contextual factors (scope and audience, authority and reputation)
• content of the source (coverage, accuracy and currency issues)
• format of the source (accessibility, design and ease of use).

Searching – when you search OMNI/NMAP you search the descriptions, keywords and titles of the resources, as described by OMNI.

You are not searching the resources themselves. The results of your search are presented as thumbnail descriptions of the resources themselves, and you can then decide whether you want to access the site, given the description provided.

The gateways can be searched using a variety of search methods (keywords, phrase searching and field searching). You can also use the operators AND, OR and NOT (*see* the section on how search engines work on page 28). Extensive online help is provided.

Funding – OMNI/NMAP is a non-profitmaking operation, based in the University of Nottingham. It has no shareholders or similar benefactors, and all of the income that it generates goes back into the development of the services that it provides.

Training – OMNI/NMAP can provide training workshops and similar events on request.

Contributions – OMNI/NMAP relies on the efforts of paid and unpaid content providers for enlarging and updating the database of unbiased, high-quality, Internet-based resources that are of relevance to the wider medical, biomedical and health communities in the UK.

OMNI and NMAP are part of a larger entity known as BIOME.[34] BIOME will provide access to quality resources in agriculture, food science, forestry, pharmaceutical sciences, medicine, nursing, dentistry, biological research, veterinary sciences, the natural world, botany and zoology. BIOME itself receives funding from higher education sources and is part of an ambitious bid to deliver a robust infrastructure for online content – the Resource Discovery Network.

Both OMNI and NMAP are examples of how gateways can help to facilitate access to credible information sources.

Search engines: a last resort?

You can see from Table 2.1 that Internet search sites are relegated to the last row. The vast majority of web pages have not been subject to any form of quality control. Standards for health information have been developed, and the Health on the Net Foundation[35] (HON) has established a 'code of conduct' which specifies eight principles of publishing on the Internet.[36] Sites can apply to be badged by HON, but few web pages adhere to these standards.

Another irony dealt by the Internet is the proliferation of 'rating' systems. These systems may be of questionable validity and reliability, and may do more harm than good if used inappropriately.[37]

One possible solution would be self-labelling of medical information by web authors, combined with the systematic appraisal of health information by users and third parties using a controlled vocabulary of terms. Labelling and filtering technologies such as the Platform for Internet Content Selection (PICS) could be utilised by Internet users searching for quality criteria.[38] These systems offer at least a potential means of rating medical content.

Until the use of such systems is more widespread and has undergone proper evaluation, the appraisal of Internet information will remain the responsibility of practitioners, medical societies and associations. Hence our downgrading of search sites when searching for evidence, and the promotion of institutions such as the Cochrane Collaboration and other sources of secondary literature.

However, search engines clearly play an important role generally within the Internet, and an understanding of how they work will help to broaden our understanding of search methodology.

How search engines work

A search engine is the name given to a piece of software that scurries around the Web reading and indexing material. The material retrieved is made available to the enquirer in two different ways. Many search engines create vast indexes of all of the material that is read by the software. The search engine will match the characters typed by the enquirer to words in the index. Another type of resource employed by these sites is a directory of sites organised by subject matter. This enables you to move from general to more specific information. For instance, you might click on 'Health' as a subject heading, and then on 'Nursing' to find particular sites of professional nursing bodies.

Ways of using search engines

There are different types of search strategy that you can use, and knowing how these search engines work will optimise the time you spend using them.

Keyword search

Most of us have used keywords to look up items on databases of some kind. Because the size of these databases is relatively small compared with the items indexed by an Internet search engine, we may have found what we were looking for by chance rather than by design.

If I was interested in pain management and tentatively typed in that phrase, the result of the search would be all of the pages that contained any of the words I had specified. Some of these might include the phrase as I typed it, but many others would be retrieved simply because the words 'pain' or 'management' were found by the search engine. Thus I would obtain 'Why Mondays are a pain' and features on 'time management'.

The search engine will rank some of these items above others. Thus if it found pain and management on the same page, these would be ranked above items where these words were separated. Items where these words were found within the same phrase would rank even higher. However, this still means that you will obtain articles like 'No pain, no gain, say management consultants'.

Phrase search

The search engine may allow you to use an exact phrase search so that only the words you typed, in the exact order you typed them in, will be retrieved. This is an option to consider when you are trying to reduce the number of search items and manage the number of leads you might want to follow up.

Logical operators or Boolean search

Boolean operators are named after the English mathematician George Boole (1815–1864). They are words that the search engine recognises as link phrases. The operators AND and NOT have the effect of narrowing a search, while the OR operator expands the search.

The problem with this exceptionally powerful method is that people often misuse the terms. For instance, suppose that you keep dogs and cats as pets and want to find out information on how to look after them properly. Typing in cats AND dogs would only return items in which *both* animals are mentioned on the same page. Often people do not understand why the results of the search are disappointing, and they reach the conclusion that the information does not exist on the Web. The OR in Boolean terms is an inclusive 'or', and returns pages containing either the word 'cats' or the word 'dogs'. If you typed in 'cats NOT dogs', then only pages with the word 'cats' would be retrieved.

Some search engine experts have advocated relegating the use of Boolean searching to areas of a site for advanced searchers.[39] Others advocate using alternative ways of doing the same thing – for example, using the mathematical symbols + to add, – to subtract and quotation marks to 'multiply', thereby forcing the search engine to match the terms exactly as they appear within the quotation marks.[40]

Concept search

Some search engines are capable of concept searching. This means that they are capable of recognising that certain words appear in certain contexts (e.g. WebTop.com).[41]

Natural language

Some search engines use natural language as an interface (e.g. Ask Jeeves).[42]

Box 2.7 Why using search engines can be problematic

Research by Steve Lawrence and C Lee Miles[43-45] at the NEC Research Institute has helped to highlight the strengths and weaknesses of search engines.

Limitations of coverage
Search engines index only a fraction of the Web, and the coverage of any one engine alone is significantly limited. No engine indexes more than about one-third of the publicly indexable Web. Although the amount of information that can be accessed with search engines is increasing, the relative coverage is decreasing because the size of the Web is increasing even faster.

Delays with updates
Even major search engines take months to update new or modified sites.

Indexing patterns vary
Commercial sites are more likely to be indexed than educational sites. Sites with large numbers of links are more likely to be indexed by search engines. US sites are more likely to be indexed than non-US sites (although Alta Vista[46] was an exception).

Poor uptake of keyword tags
Only 34% of home pages used the simple HTML function of 'keywords' and descriptive 'metatags'. An authoritative standard for indexing, known as the Dublin Core metadata standard, was only used by 0.3% of sites in the study.

How you can use this research to produce better search strategies
Use several search engines
If you need to use search sites, do not rely on one alone, but make use of several search engines. Combining six search engines covered 3.5 times as much of the Web as one engine on average – about twice the coverage of the best-performing search engine.

Recency
The same method can be used to offset the problems caused by delays in the time it takes for new pages to be added or old pages modified.

Which combination?
The major search engines are better for information that is more difficult to find, more up to date information and comprehensiveness (e.g. Alta Vista, Excite,[47] HotBot,[48] Fast Search,[49] Lycos[50] and Northern Light[51]). For popular information a directory such as Yahoo![52] and engines such as Google[53] and DirectHit[54] are often useful. Metasearch engines have the advantage of scanning more than one search engine, so these might figure in a planned search. They include MetaCrawler,[55] ProFusion,[56] SurfWax[57] and Copernic.[58]

Use a specialised search engine where appropriate
Because specialised search engines have a narrower focus they have fewer pages to index, and are therefore more easily managed and kept up to date.

Summary

Formulating questions and undertaking online searches are two of the most important skills to acquire.

The components of a clinical question are:

- the patient/problem
- the intervention or manoeuvre
- the outcome.

Scientific literature can be classified as primary or secondary.

- Primary literature refers to articles about original research.
- Secondary literature consists of synthesised evidence from original research.

Awareness of the distinction between different types of information and where they can be found online will improve your search.

- It is important to structure your search and execute a number of sub-searches if the search is to retrieve information that is timely, accurate and complete.
- Draw up a table of the resources that are most relevant to your specialty or clinical area, and use it for searches and to prioritise reliable resources.
- Resources range from subject gateways to bibliographic databases, online journals and documents, and discussion lists.
- Resources for meeting your information needs include people (via discussion lists).
- Familiarity with the retrieval methods used by search engines will improve your search.
- Using several search engines will enhance your search.

References

1 Webber S and Johnston B (2001) *Information Literacy: definitions and models.* Department of Information Studies, Sheffield University, Sheffield; http://dis.shef.ac.uk/literacy/definitions.htm

2 NHS Executive Enabling People Programme (1999) *Learning to Manage Health Information.* NHS Executive, Leeds.

3 Flanders N (1970) *Analysing Teacher Behaviour.* Addison-Wesley, London.

4 Sackett DL, Richardson WS, Rosenberg W and Haynes RB (1998) *Evidence-Based Medicine. How to practice and teach EBM.* Churchill Livingstone, Edinburgh.

5 Greenhalgh T (1997) *How to Read a Paper.* BMJ Publishing Group, London.

6 Brown SJ (1999) *Knowledge for Health Care Practice. A guide to using research evidence.* WB Saunders Company, Philadelphia, PA.

7 Institute of Medicine (1990) *Clinical Practice Guidelines.* National Academy Press, Washington, DC.

8 http://www.update-software.com/clibhome/clib.htm

9 http://www.evidence.org/

10 http://www.bmjpg.com/data/ebm.htm

11 http://www.acponline.org/journals/acpjc/jcmenu.htm

12 http://cebm.jr2.ox.ac.uk

13 http://www.hta.nhsweb.nhs.uk/

14 http://www.nice.org.uk

15 http://www.htbs.org.uk/

16 http://www.doh.gov.uk/nsf/nsfhome.htm

17 http://www.doh.gov.uk/nsf/mentalhealth.htm

18 http://www.doh.gov.uk/nsf/coronary.htm

19 http://www.doh.gov.uk/nsf/olderpeople.htm

20 http://www.doh.gov.uk/nsf/diabetes/

21 http://www.doh.gov.uk/nsf/children.htm

22 http://www.doh.gov.uk/nsf/longterm.htm

23 Shafir E and Tversky A (1992) Thinking through uncertainty: non-consequential reasoning and choice. *Cogn Psychol.* **24**: 449–74.

24 Redelmeier D, Koehler D, Liberman V and Tversky A (1995) Probability judgement in medicine: discounting unspecified possibilities. *Med Decision Making.* **15**: 227–30.

25 Gigerenzer G and Goldstein D (1996) Reasoning the fast and frugal way: models of bounded rationality. *Psychol Rev.* **103**: 650–69.

26 http://www.ncbi.nlm.nih.gov/PubMed/

27 http://www.bniplus.co.uk/

28 http://www.cinahl.com/

29 http://www.bmj.com/

30 http://highwire.stanford.edu/

31 http://www.jiscmail.ac.uk/

32 http://omni.ac.uk/

33 http://nmap.ac.uk/

34 http://biome.ac.uk/

35 http://hon.ch/

36 Boyer C, Selby M, Scherrer JR and Appel RD (1998) The Health on the Net code of conduct for medical and health websites. *Comput Biol Med.* **28**: 603–10.

37 Jadad A and Gagliardi A (1998) Rating health information on the Internet – navigating to knowledge or to Babel? *JAMA.* **279**: 611–14.

38 Eysenbach G and Diegpen T (1998) Towards quality management of medical information on the Internet: evaluation, labelling and filtering of information. *BMJ.* **28**: 603–10.

39 Nielsen J (2001) *Search: visible and simple.* Jakob Nielsen's Alertbox, 13 May 2001; http://www.useit.com/alertbox/

40 http://www.searchenginewatch.com/

41 http://www.WebTop.com

42 http://www.askjeeves.com

43 Lawrence S and Giles C (1998) Searching the World Wide Web. *Science*. **280**: 98.

44 Lawrence S and Giles L (1999) Accessibility of information on the Web. *Nature*. **400**: 107–9.

45 Lawrence S and Giles L (1999) *New Study on the Accessibility and Distribution of Information on the Web*. NEC Research Institute, Princeton, NJ.

46 http://www.altavista.com/

47 http://www.excite.com/

48 http://www.hotbot.com/

49 http://www.alltheweb.com/

50 http://lycos.com/

51 http://www.northernlight.com/

52 http://www.yahoo.com/

53 http://www.google.com/

54 http://www.directhit.com/

55 http://www.metacrawler.com/

56 http://www.profusion.com/

57 http://www.surfwax.com/

58 http://www.copernic.com/

Mapping

Organising information

If the Internet is so chaotic and mutable, how can we be expected to use it? Although the Internet poses very specific problems for students, its value as a research tool can be enhanced if we attempt to give it the structure it palpably lacks.

The precise mechanisms and processes that are used by the human mind to store and retrieve information are not fully understood. Human memory is clearly highly organised, and we seem to have an innate tendency to cluster items which we feel are related. Information is sorted in short-term or 'working memory' by interaction with knowledge in long-term memory. The limiting factor is that short-term memory can only cope with a small number of incoming items – around five to nine – at any time. Our capacity to find and process relationships is about two to three concepts in working memory.[1] There needs to be a systematic sequence of iterations between working memory and long-term memory in order to organise and integrate large bodies of knowledge.[2]

Memory experts have demonstrated that we can increase the capacity of our short-term memory by breaking down incoming information or 'chunking' it. This helps to integrate it and relate it to knowledge that is already in our long-term memory.

In one experiment, Bower and colleagues[3] asked participants to memorise a list of words. For one group the words had been organised into a conceptual hierarchy (*see* Figure 3.1). The other group was tasked to learn the same words arranged randomly. The group that was given the hierarchy recalled on average 65% of the words, whereas the other group could only recall 19% of the words on average.

Imagery forms the basis of many different types of mnemonic device or memory aid. We can use our inherent graphic and organisational abilities to improve our knowledge maintenance and learning skills.

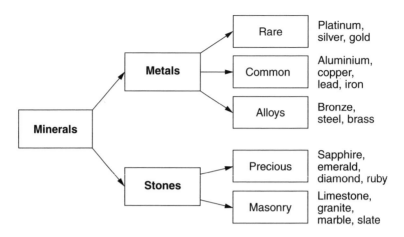

Figure 3.1 A conceptual hierarchy as used by Bower *et al.*[3]

Box 3.1 Using imagery to assist memory: Simonides and the 'method of loci'

Verbal material is remembered more efficiently if it can be associated with a visual image. Cicero[4] told the story of the Greek poet Simonides, who had mastered a way of improving memory by using a visualising technique. Simonides had attended a banquet and had the good fortune to have left early before the roof of the hall caved in, killing most of the occupants. Because identification proved impossible, the poet was asked if he could remember all of the guests he had seen. Simonides was able to recall every person and where they were sitting. He used a method of associating each guest with an image, and was able to use this spatial map to 'walk through' the banqueting hall, placing each guest within it. In ancient Greece this 'method of loci' was regarded as the best technique for learning.

We all use maps

We are all born map readers. As Dennis Wood[5] has explained, every child who looks at the endpapers of *Winnie the Pooh*[6] can find their way around Christopher Robin's domain, and knows where each of the characters lives in relation to the others without prompting. Similarly, we can sail with the crew in *Swallows and Amazons*[7] and trek across the Wilderland with Bilbo Baggins.[8] The terrain may change, and the sophistication of the representation may change, but the map is understood.

Any map – from a child's treasure map to a satellite weather map – is an interpretative framework which uses a set of (sometimes elaborate) conventions which we need to be able to decode in order to understand it. The map sets up rules and manipulates a minimum of three cartographic codes of projection, ratio and symbolisation. Consider the case of symbolisation. Typographic marks can be used to equate with anything that the map maker wishes (e.g. a river, a mountain, an area of low pressure, spread of HIV virus or the retreat of Napoleon's armies from Russia in 1812).

Maps are effective and can be relied upon. Consider another example. You can travel to a foreign country not knowing a word of the language, and you can still negotiate a city's underground system provided that you have a map. You do not need to be told that the map is not to scale, or that this line does not really run straight through the city, or that the sinuous blue line represents the river running through it. All you need to understand is that the underground map is an elegant representation of a network, providing the traveller with all of the information that they need to get from A to B.

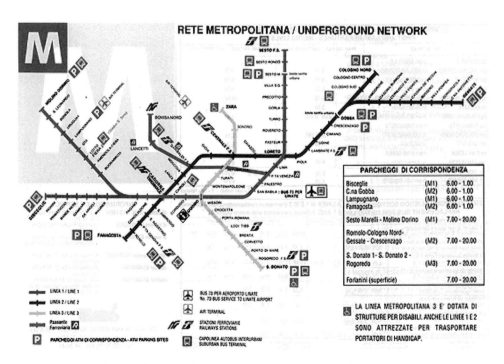

Figure 3.2 Map of the Milan underground system.[9]

Making maps work for us

Our underground rail route map, whether it be of the system beneath Milan, Paris or London, represents a network. The Internet is also a network – a point so obvious that it is almost overlooked. Websites can be envisaged as nodes on a map. If we can find a way of representing this fact, we may be able to use the power of the map to meet our information needs. If mapping can perform the topological conjuring trick of transforming a complex entity such as a metropolitan underground system into a plane (the two-dimensional map), then the same metamorphosis should be feasible with sections of the Web.

Smart maps

We started using 'smart maps' as part of the office routines of an information service specialising in quality improvement and clinical effectiveness issues. These maps were developed as a means of building responses to frequently asked questions. We needed a way of formulating a common approach to answering enquiries without it becoming too inflexible. Smart maps only become inhibiting when they are considered to be 'finished'. Their main value is as a tool to begin the process of defining the resources that are required to meet a particular information need.

Box 3.2 explains how you can build your own thematic maps or smart maps.

Building meta-knowledge

Mapping techniques will help us to get orientated in the bewildering information landscape. The selectivity of the map will screen out much of the noise and distractions that are inherent in Web-based searches. By focusing on an area of interest we can reduce the risk of defensive avoidance and hypervigilance described in Chapter 1. The map should encourage vigilance – the optimum state. It is an adaptive tool for learning, helping us to monitor changes in the sites of interest and guarding against the attrition of content on the Web.

Box 3.2 Build your own smart map

What is a smart map?
A smart map consists of a question and a list of information resources that can be used in order to answer that question.

What hardware/software do I need to begin with?
If you have access to the Internet and a word-processing package that recognises hypertext links (e.g. Word 97), you can begin to devise your own smart map.

Where do I start?
Start with the question. What is the focus of your question? Have you considered any of the following?

- Clinical outcome.
- Intervention or treatment.
- Preventative or diagnostic action.
- Patient experience.
- Population.
- Associated factors such as attitudes and beliefs.
- Setting or time factors.

How do I find out about information on the Internet?
Talk to information specialists about the resources that might help you in your search. It is likely that there will be some resources (e.g. bibliographic databases or other relevant sites) that will be available online. Take time to note these down.

How do I group things?
Group the sites into different clusters according to relevant categories (e.g. by resource type – sources of systematic reviews, critically appraised topics, newsgroups, etc.).

How do I know that the smart map will work?
Type out your sites and put them in boxes according to the different categories you have given them. Type in the Internet addresses for each site. A site address should automatically turn blue when your word-processing package has recognised it as a hypertext link.

What are the benefits?
Mapping out sites in this way makes it easier to gain a quick overview of a subject area. You might make several attempts to develop a map. You can delete or add sites and update the map, and you can use it to help you to adjust the focus of your question.
   Above all you can share your map with others, either by photo-copying it or by sending it by traditional 'snail mail' or, ideally, sending it as an email attachment.

What kinds of resources are available online to support evidence-based practice?

Evidence

Secondary sources (guidelines, systematic reviews, etc.)
Cochrane Library
http://www.update-software.com/clibhome/clib.htm
Effective Health Care bulletins
http://www.york.ac.uk/inst/crd/
Health Evidence bulletins – Wales
http://www.uwcm.ac.uk/uwcm/lb/pep
Health technology appraisal
National Service Frameworks
    http://www.doh.gov.uk/nsf/nsfhome.htm
NICE http://www.nice.org.uk
SIGN http://www.sign.ac.uk/

Primary sources (primary research, bibliographic)
MEDLINE http://www.ncbi.nlm.nih.gov/PubMed/
National Research Register http://www.update-software.com/nrronline/NRROPEN.htm

Meta-searching secondary and primary sources
SUMsearch http://sumsearch.uthscsa.edu/

Gateways

Organisations
NeLH http://www.nelh.nhs.uk/

TRIAGE
http://www.shef.ac.uk/~scharr/triage/

TRIP http://www.tripdatabase.com/

Instruction sites

General introduction
Centre for Evidence-based Medicine
http://cebm.jr2.ox.ac.uk

Teaching and learning resources for evidence-based practice – University of Middlesex
http://www.mdx.ac.uk/www.retsh/ebp/main.html

Critical appraisal
WISDOM http://www.wisdomnet.co.uk/

Searching
http://www.nthames-health.tpmde.ac.uk/evidence_strategies/index.htm

Discussion groups

Networks
CHAIN http://www.open.gov.uk/doh/ntrd/chain/chain.htm
EBM http://www.jiscmail.ac.uk/lists/evidence-based-health/
Systematic reviews http://www.jiscmail.ac.uk/lists/sys-review/

This Smart Map was last updated on:

Figure 3.3   A smart map.

Applications

Smart maps are adaptable and can be applied to any subject matter. They could be used as primers for broader subject areas, but are equally useful for more specific searches.

Maps should be regularly checked for the following:

• substantive change in the content of the site – if a site unveils new content, this might warrant changes to the map

- omissions – sites can be added or deleted
- link rot – changes to the site address or the complete disappearance of the site/page
- recency – all maps are time sensitive, and we should adhere to our code of conduct for maintaining the accuracy of material by date stamping the map.

You could use smart maps within a simple library set up on a networked computer or on your own PC. Remember that you can send the smart map as an attachment to an email.

Advantages

Smart maps pass our test for fast and frugal heuristics. The use of hyper-links speeds up the computation time and provides an efficient means of accessing important material. The mapping of sites has several advantages over simply bookmarking 'favourites' in a directory.

Smart maps introduce a more proactive approach to intelligence gathering when you are conducting searches on the Web. Themes can be explored and analysed, and these maps encourage the researcher to think in terms of questions and subquestions or areas and subareas for study. Maps can be used as the springboard for one's own guided searches. They could also form part of a study programme.

Further mapping techniques

Two other mapping techniques can assist us at various stages of informa-tion research. *Concept maps*[1] and *mind maps*[10] will be used throughout the remaining chapters of this book. Both methods are tools for organising and representing knowledge.

Concept maps

Concept maps are interpretable pictorial views of concepts and how these are interrelated. Concepts are defined as 'perceived regularities' in events or things within a particular context. They are represented on the map as labelled circles or boxes of some type. A connecting line between two or more concepts indicates propositions, or the relationship between con-cepts. Propositions containing concepts are connected with words to form meaningful statements.

Figure 3.4 shows a concept map of some of the ideas contained within this chapter. The minimal use of text makes it much easier for the eye to scan the page. The visual representation becomes a flexible tool for communicating quite complex ideas in a holistic fashion.

Concept maps are usually presented in a hierarchical manner, with broader concepts at the top of the map and more specific concepts lower down. Smart maps and concept maps share the characteristic of focusing on a particular question or exploring a particular context.

The other important feature to note is the use of cross-links. The cross-links make the connections between segments of the map explicit. It is the creation of a hierarchical structure coupled with the imaginative linking of concepts that gives concept mapping its unique ability to enhance learning and test understanding.

Applications

Concept maps have a number of applications. They are helpful for group work and can be used to capture ideas from brainstorming sessions. They are becoming increasingly popular both as learning tools and as problem-solving tools. Teachers can use them to diagnose student misconceptions and to test the understanding of basic concepts. Because of the structural correspondence between concept maps and hypertext design, they have been used as design tools for hypertext documents.

We could use concept maps to help us at various points of the research cycle. They can be particularly helpful at the inception of a project, when it is important to gain a grasp of the key features of a topic before any searching has been done.

In Figure 3.5 we have applied the technique to present a visual summary of the recommendations from the Royal College of Nursing guideline on the recognition and assessment of acute pain in children.[11] A concept map can give a bird's-eye view of the scope and contents of the guideline.

Clinicians often complain about the bulk and complexity of clinical guidelines. These are typically published in several formats, including technical reports, patient versions and summary documents.[12] Visual representations of guideline recommendations (e.g. flow diagrams) have been used, but are still uncommon.[13]

Concept maps can collapse and compact complex documents into one side of paper. If concept maps were used to summarise the content of clinical guidelines, clinicians would have the fastest possible access to the knowledge domain.

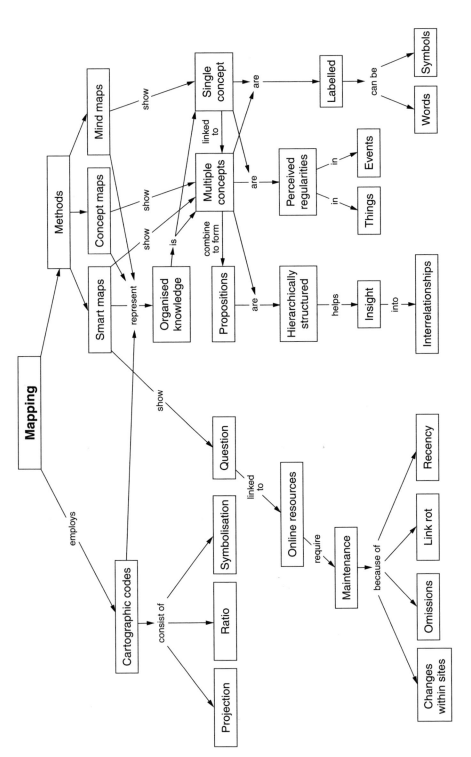

Figure 3.4 Concept map for the mapping chapter.

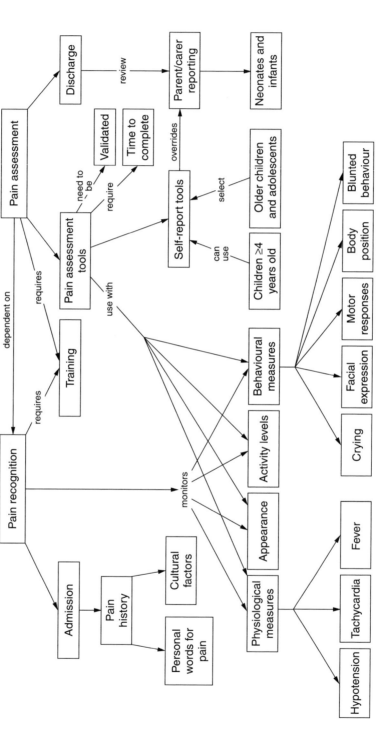

Figure 3.5 Concept map for the recognition and assessment of acute pain in children.

Mind maps

Tony Buzan[14] developed mind mapping after conducting research into note-taking techniques. A mind map consists of a central word or concept, from which branches are drawn radiating outward to other ideas relating to that word. These main branches are labelled, and these 'child words' can branch again into subtopics. Colour and arrows are used to show connections and to highlight relationships. The main difference between mind maps and concept maps is that mind maps always focus on one central concept, whereas concept maps tend to display multiple concepts. Concept maps are really networks, whereas mind maps branch like trees.

You might find mind mapping particularly useful when formulating your research question (*see* Figure 3.6).

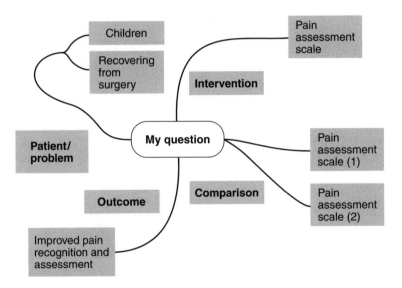

Figure 3.6   Using mind maps to formulate questions.

We have used the PICO mnemonic, discussed in Chapter 2, inside our mind map. The four main branches radiating from the central question are labelled after the elements of PICO. Each branch can then be used to explore issues within that branch, or to focus your thinking about each one. Here the question pertains to researching the best pain assessment tool for children who are recovering from surgery.

Mind mapping is often used to facilitate creative thinking and to explore the different perceptions and possible misunderstandings of a particular concept within a team. For example, it could be used to explore different perceptions of 'clinical governance'. We have used this technique to present overviews of the content within each of the clinical subject areas that follow in subsequent chapters. You will find a mind map prefacing the chapters on mental health, child health, care of the elderly and primary care.

Summary

Maps use conventions which we all seem to be able to understand, and they are a tool that we all have some experience of using.

- Maps are selective.
- They serve interests.
- They represent the world.

We can use the power of maps to improve our knowledge of the Internet. Smart maps represent one way in which we can use maps to help us.

- Smart maps are intended to meet specific information needs. They are *selective*.
- They use hyperlinks to represent nodes on the Internet. They are *efficient*.
- They can be easily copied, updated and shared between members of a team. They are *transferable*.
- They provide a means of combating information overload, improving our meta-knowledge and enhancing the learning process. They promote *vigilance*.

Concept maps and mind maps are tools for organising and representing knowledge graphically. Mind maps present a central concept and related topics radiating from it, whereas concept maps present several concepts and represent the relationships between them.

References

1 Novak JD (2000) The theory underlying concept maps and how to construct them; http://cmap.coginst.uwf.edu/info/printer.html

2 Anderson OR (1992) Some interrelationships between constructivist models of learning and current neurobiological theory, with implications for science education. *J Res Sci Teaching*. **29**: 1037–58.

3 Bower GH, Clark MC, Lesgold A and Winsenz D (1969) Hierarchical retrieval schemes in recall of categorical word lists. *J Verbal Learn Verbal Behav*. **8**: 323–43.

4   Yates FA (1974) *The Art of Memory.* University of Chicago Press, Chicago.

5   Wood D (1992) *The Power of Maps.* Guildford Press, New York.

6   Milne AA (1926) *Winnie the Pooh.* Methuen & Co., London.

7   Ransome A (1930) *Swallows and Amazons.* Jonathan Cape, London.

8   Tolkien JRR (1937) *The Hobbit.* Houghton Mifflin, London.

9   http://www.sea-aeroportmilano.it/images/Maps/mm.gif

10 http://www.mind-map.com

11 Royal College of Nursing Institute (2000) *The Recognition and Assessment of Acute Pain in Children: technical report.* Royal College of Nursing Institute, London.

12 http://www.nice.org.uk

13 http://www.eguidelines.co.uk

14 Buzan T (1995) *The Mindmap Book* (2e). BBC Books, London.

Care of older people

Lesley Overall

Britain's getting older. The number of people aged over 65 has doubled in the last 70 years. The number of people over 90 will double in the next 25 years.[1]

This statement introduces the Department of Health's National Service Framework for Older People, published in March 2001, which is a response to one of the most challenging problems facing the health service as we enter the next millennium, namely the need to improve and expand healthcare services for the burgeoning elderly population.

It is difficult to predict what systems of care will be required, but it is clear that the majority of it will be away from hospitals providing critical care, diagnostics and tertiary care. Much of it will be organised by Care Trusts in the community and will come under the all-embracing term of *intermediate care* (for a discussion of this, *see* the notes of the conference on *Intermediate Care: the Evidence Base in Practice*, held at the Royal College of Physicians).[2]

Secondary sources of evidence

Evidence-based clinical practice guidelines

Recommendations within the National Service Framework are underpinned by evidence from a range of publications, including clinical practice guidelines. One of the main sources for guidance on best practice is the National Institute for Clinical Excellence (NICE).[3] Three guidelines relevant to 'older people's services' are contained within the 2000/2001 NICE guideline programme,[4] namely *Risk Assessment and Prevention of Pressure Sores* (2001) and *Management of Venous Leg Ulcers* (1998), both produced by the Royal College of Nursing,[5] and *Non-Insulin-Dependent Diabetes* (2000),

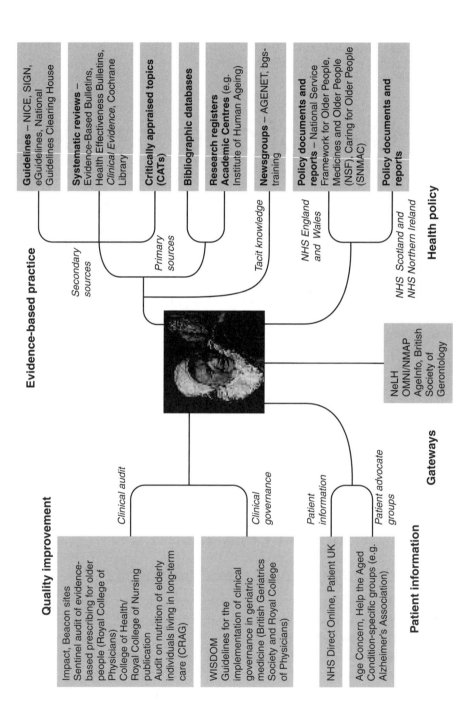

Evidence-based practice

Guidelines – NICE, SIGN, eGuidelines, National Guidelines Clearing House

Systematic reviews – Evidence-Based Bulletins, Health Effectiveness Bulletins, *Clinical Evidence*, Cochrane Library

Critically appraised topics (CATs)

Bibliographic databases

Research registers Academic Centres (e.g. Institute of Human Ageing)

Newsgroups – AGENET, bgs-training

Policy documents and reports – National Service Framework for Older People, Medicines and Older People (NSF), Caring for Older People (SNMAC)

Policy documents and reports

Health policy

Secondary sources

Primary sources

Tacit knowledge

NHS England and Wales

NHS Scotland and NHS Northern Ireland

NeLH OMNI/NMAP AgeInfo, British Society of Gerontology

Gateways

Quality improvement

Impact, Beacon sites Sentinel audit of evidence-based prescribing for older people (Royal College of Physicians) College of Health/ Royal College of Nursing publication Audit on nutrition of elderly individuals living in long-term care (CRAG)

WiSDOM Guidelines for the implementation of clinical governance in geriatric medicine (British Geriatrics Society and Royal College of Physicians)

Clinical audit

Clinical governance

Patient information

Patient advocate groups

NHS Direct Online, Patient UK

Age Concern, Help the Aged Condition-specific groups (e.g. Alzheimer's Association)

Patient information

Figure 4.1 Site map for care of older people.

produced by the Royal College of General Practitioners.[6] The NICE guideline programme announced in 2001 includes prevention of falls as a topic.[7]

Further important sources of guidelines relating to older people are those produced by the Scottish Intercollegiate Guidelines Network (SIGN).[8] SIGN has published two guidelines targeted at particular aspects of care relating to the older person. These are *Hypertension in Older People* (January 2001) and *Management of Elderly Patients with Fractured Hip* (July 1997). However, because older people are often afflicted with a number of medical problems, contained within SIGN's guideline programme are subjects that could also relate to the care of the older person, such as dementia, leg ulcers and stroke.

There are three UK collections of clinical guidelines worth bookmarking for a quick overview of guidelines relevant to care of the elderly. The Clinical Effectiveness Evaluation Unit at the Royal College of Physicians has a searchable guidelines database.[9] It has several collections that allow quick access to relevant material, including one on *Healthcare of Older People*. The National electronic Library for Health[10] is developing a database of clinical practice guidelines. Medendium's database on eGuidelines[11] for primary care can be searched. These summaries of guidelines are only available to healthcare professionals, but can be accessed quite easily after registering a user name and password.

Guidelines for the Prevention of Falls in People Over 65, produced by St Bartholomew's and the Royal London Medical School (Department of General Practice and Primary Care) can be viewed via the *British Medical Journal* online.[12]

Guidelines exist for other related topics, such as stroke, hypertension and dementia. Therefore the following organisations are also important sources to access.

- The British Association for Parenteral and Enteral Nutrition has published *Guidelines for the Detection and Management of Malnutrition in the Community* (2000).[13]
- The Stroke Association's guideline, with recommendations from the Royal College of Physicians, *National Clinical Guidelines for Stroke* (2001).[14] The Clinical Resource Efficiency Support Team (CREST), a group consisting of 17 health professionals from the health service in Northern Ireland, has produced a guideline entitled: *Consensus Guidance on the Management of Acute Stroke* (1999).[15]
- The Royal College of General Practitioners has produced a guideline on *Coronary Heart Disease*.[16]
- The University of Newcastle Centre for Health Services Research, North of England Evidence-Based Guideline Development Project's guideline on *Primary Care Management of Dementia*.[17]

- A collaboration between the British Medical Association, the Resuscitation Council and the Royal College of Nursing has led to a joint statement being issued that gives guidance on *Decisions Relating to Cardiopulmonary Resuscitation* (2001). These guidelines can be found at the Resuscitation Council's website.[18]

Outside the UK, the National Guidelines Clearing House (NGC)[19] provides a searchable database of evidence-based clinical practice guidelines. The NGC is operated by the US Department of Health and the Human Services Agency for Healthcare Research and Quality. The guidelines held on the database have met certain criteria – they have been published since 1995, they are written in English, and they have used an explicit and robust development methodology.

Systematic reviews and critically appraised topics

The Cochrane Collaboration, which is an international network of individuals, maintains and disseminates systematic reviews of the effects of healthcare interventions. Access to the Cochrane Library[20] is restricted to healthcare professionals via registration and use of a password.

Contained within the Cochrane Collaboration is the Cochrane Health Care of Older People Field.[21] Listed in this section, which can be found via the Cochrane Library fields section, are details of the scope and topics covered. These embrace 'evidence concerning treatment of healthcare problems of older adults, including but not limited to delirium, dementia, incontinence, cardiovascular diseases, healthcare outcomes, hazards of hospitalisation, falls and their sequelae, long-term care and osteoporosis'. The following keywords can be used to locate these references to the older person: ageing, aged, elderly, elder, geriatric, geriatrics, gerontology and gerontological, combined with the clinical topic.

The NHS Centre for Reviews and Dissemination (CRD) is based at the University of York.[22] It promotes the use of research-based knowledge by maintaining databases of research reviews, economic evaluations of healthcare and abstracts of technology assessments. CRD publications include *Effective Health Care Bulletins*, *Effectiveness Matters* and *CRD Reports*. Many of these topics are relevant to the care of older people.

Health Evidence Bulletins – Wales,[23] produced by the University of Wales, is a collaborative project involving health authorities, providers of primary and secondary healthcare and library and information units. These bulletins act as 'signposts' to the best current evidence across a broad range of evidence types and subject areas, including cancer, cardiovascular disease, respiratory disease, injury prevention, learning disabilities, oral health and mental health. The only drawback is that it may be necessary to view every bulletin listed, as references to older people may be contained in any of the subject areas mentioned above. For example, contained within the 'injury prevention' bulletin, references can be found to the older person.[24]

Critically appraised topics are available from the Centre for Evidence-Based Medicine in Oxford. Their CAT bank[25] is accessible via the Internet. There are two ways in which a search can be conducted on this database – either by browsing the list of topics, or by entering a term in the search box. For example, by 'browsing', a number of references are found that apply to the care of older people, not necessarily with the term 'older people' contained within them. Alternatively, by using the search box and entering the phrase 'older people', nothing is found, but by entering the term 'elderly' five references are located.

The *Clinical Evidence*[26] compendium is now available online as well as in book form via subscription. *Clinical Evidence* covers the most common or most important conditions in primary and hospital care, and is intended as an aid to clinical decision making (medical, surgical, nursing and complementary interventions). The online version has many features that make it a useful search tool. It has a list of subject categories, a contents box for general searching which also provides links to other databases (MEDLINE and Cochrane), and a glossary. Although there is not a specific category for the 'older person', a search under this term will retrieve a number of relevant references. The NeLH offers the complete online version of *Clinical Evidence* to all NHS employees who register with it.

The *Bandolier*[27] site also provides a searchable resource of CATs and reviews of research evidence. It has collected those references relating to older people and subdivided them into the following sections: drugs and vaccines; skin and nails; hips, knees and arthritis; eyes; laxatives; dementia; exercise; and a miscellaneous file.

The Aggressive Research Intelligence Facility (ARIF)[28] is an evidence-finding facility based at the University of Birmingham. The unit provides an archive of research information uncovered in response to requests from organisations in the West Midlands. You can read the response to the following question. 'What are the effects/effectiveness of interventions to promote health, prevent disease and rehabilitate older patients?'

The British Geriatrics Society[29] offers what it calls a compendium index, in which it has collated evidence for the effectiveness or otherwise of inter-ventions for older people. For example, one compendium document is on the evidence of effectiveness in assisting the purchasing of general rehabilitation and specific packages for rehabilitation of stroke and fractured neck of femur.

Primary sources of evidence

PubMed[30] provides free access to bibliographic information that includes MEDLINE as well as additional life science journals. It covers the fields of medicine, nursing, dentistry and the healthcare system, although it has an American bias. The references contained in the database provide basic citation information, but a number of them have abstracts that can be downloaded or just viewed.

The two easiest ways of searching PubMed are by Medical Subject Heading (MeSH) and by Limits searching (e.g. search limited to age group, publication date and type, language and gender, among other category limits). For example, when using the MeSH browser a number of references under the terms 'older people' or 'older adult' will be displayed. However, if too many items are retrieved, the Limits search will be the best search option. A PubMed search can also have combined, cross-referenced search terms, such as 'older people' AND 'nutrition', which can lead to the retrieval of more specific references.

Two other bibliographical databases with free access that are important searching tools for references to the older person are the online version of the *British Medical Journal (BMJ)*,[31] and the English National Board for Nursing and Health Visiting (ENB).[32]

The *British Medical Journal (BMJ)* contains full text articles published in the weekly *BMJ* from 1994 until the present day. References can be obtained by undertaking a search using keywords or by selecting the 'collected resources' section which lists a collection of *BMJ* articles that have been arranged by specialty and topic. In addition, this database is very useful for obtaining information relating to other reference sources.

The English Nursing Board (ENB) is a non-departmental public body which fulfils the statutory functions set out in the Nurses, Midwives and Health Visitors Act 1997. Its database searches a range of journals that are of special relevance to nursing in the UK. Apart from journals, it indexes other sources, including research/reports and briefings from various organisations, such as the King's Fund. Help with the best ways of searching this database and the list of the journals that it indexes can be found when you click on to the database section from the main menu.

Other sources of primary evidence can be found on the National Research Register (NRR).[33] This is a register of ongoing and recently completed research projects funded by or of interest to the UK's National Health Service. The National Research Register holds details of over 72 000 research projects. Therefore, when searching for items on the older adult, a large number of references will be returned unless the search enquiry is refined.

A more manageable database for viewing or searching is the Department of Health's Research Findings electronic Register (ReFeR).[34] ReFer contains summaries of research findings from single primary research studies as well as systematic reviews of primary studies from the NHS Research and Development Programme and the Department of Health Policy Research Programme. It is freely accessible and can easily be searched by entering a keyword or phrase. The results can be viewed and downloaded by title or in full text. It is a useful database to use, as the results of a search can act as a 'signpost' to other related research.

Research-active organisations in the field of gerontology include the Centre for Policy in Ageing.[35] This organisation has an information service about old age and ageing called AgeInfo, consisting of a database of books, articles, reports, organisations and events. The Age Concern Institute of Gerontology[36] at King's College London provides the Gerontology Data Service (GDS). This gives support to research into the elderly population and publishes research tools such as the Scales Database of research assessment instruments specifically designed for use with elderly people. The Institute of Human Ageing[37] at the University of Liverpool has developed the Geriatric Mental State Interview, and information about the use of this research instrument can be found at their site.

For a more extensive list of gerontology research centres around the world, refer to the Social Science Information Gateway[38] (*see* Box 4.1).

Box 4.1 Older People Section on Social Science Information Gateway

The Social Science Information Gateway (SOSIG)[38] has a useful collection of Internet resources. The listing is grouped by type of resource, such as 'articles/papers/reports' followed by bibliographic databases, and so on. Click on one of the items from the list and you will be able to read a description of the item.

The listings have a global perspective on the subject and include items from the USA, Canada, Australia and Europe. The research centres and societies listings are extensive. The site has a link to the *Merck Manual of Geriatrics* under its book section.

The Older People section of SOSIG is under the editorship of the National Institute for Social Work at the University of Bradford.

Tacit knowledge

Discussion groups dedicated to care of the elderly include AgeNet[39] and bgs-training.[40] You can obtain more information about the second list from the British Geriatrics Society website.[41]

Networks and newsgroups are often a good way of making contacts, seeking advice or sharing experiences with other professionals who are working in the same area of healthcare. From the multidisciplinary network CHAIN[42] you can access their directory and receive targeted information on conferences, educational events, research opportunities and much more.

Policy in the four countries

The most recent development of the Government's intentions to radically improve the health service in England is the NHS Plan.[43] Details of the plan were unveiled in July 2000, setting out measures over the next ten years for putting patients and people first, and for increasing funding for the health service over the next five years.

National Service Frameworks are the 'blueprints' for defining how services are best provided and to what standards. The *National Service Framework for Older People*[1] sets out a programme of action on how to improve health and social care services for older people. The main standards of care covered are rooting out age discrimination (standard 1), person-centred care (standard 2), intermediate care (standard 3), general hospital care (standard 4), stroke (standard 5), falls (standard 6), mental health in older people (standard 7) and the promotion of health and active life in older age (standard 8).

Another document, the *National Minimum Standards for Care Homes for Older People*,[44] will set out core requirements to ensure that the accommodation provided for older people meets their needs. These standards are published by the Secretary of State for Health in accordance with Section 23 of the Care Standards Act 2000 (CSA). They replace the 1984 Registered Homes Act and applied from April 2002. The Care Standards Act creates the National Care Standards Commission[45] (NCSC), an independent non-governmental public body, to regulate social and healthcare services previously regulated by local councils and health authorities.

Another valuable resource is the Department of Health's publication *The Essence of Care: Patient-Focused Benchmarking for Health Care Practitioners*.[46] It is described in the foreword by Sarah Mullally, the Chief Nursing Officer, as 'a practical toolkit for nurses and others. It focuses on those core and essential aspects of care that quite rightly matter so much to patients and their carers'. *The Essence of Care* contains benchmarking tools related to eight aspects of care, namely principles of self-care, food and nutrition, personal and oral hygiene, continence and bladder and bowel care, pressure ulcers, record keeping, safety of clients/patients with mental health needs in acute mental health and general hospital settings, and privacy and dignity.

Further Government guidance that is applicable to the care of older adults consists of a review of continence services entitled *Good Practice in Continence Services*.[47] This guidance sets out a 'model of good practice', and its key aims are to raise awareness among professionals of the problems of continence, to provide practical guidance for the NHS on the organisation of continence services across primary, acute and tertiary care, to provide advice on the individual assessment and treatment of continence by primary care and community staff, and to describe targets that can be developed locally. This review also gives details of other key documents relating to continence services, in particular the RCN guide aimed at the nurse specialist (*Commissioning Continence Advisory Services*, published by the Royal College of Nursing in 2000).[47]

The Clinical Resource Efficiency Support Team (CREST)[48] in Northern Ireland publishes guidelines, clinical audit projects and service standards across a range of topics. Current working areas that may impinge on care of the elderly include screening for hypertension and diabetes care in Northern Ireland.

Details of health priorities for older people in Scotland were published in *Our National Health: a Plan for Action, a Plan for Change*.[49] This and many other documents and reports on the progress of the plan are available from Scottish Health on the Web. The Scottish Health Advisory Service (SHAS) has published quality indicators for older people's services, and these will underpin the work of SHAS in its role as an inspectorate, evaluating and advising older people's services in Scotland.[50] The Social Work Services Inspectorate of the Scottish Executive is working on standards for older people who are residing in care homes.[51]

The National Assembly for Wales website for the NHS Plan is called *Improving Health in Wales – a Plan for the NHS and its Partners*.[52] One project that will impact on the provision of care for the elderly is *Tackling CHD in Wales: Implementing Through Evidence*, which is available through the Health of Wales Information Service (HOWIS).[53]

Gateways

Organising Medical Networked Information (OMNI)[54] is compiled by a core team of information specialists and subject experts based at the University of Nottingham Greenfield Medical Library, in partnership with health librarians and information specialists from a range of organisations. The sources are selected for their quality and relevance, and are regularly updated. By undertaking a simple search on OMNI, references to other organisations, journals and reviews can be followed up. A sister database, NMAP,[55] is aimed at Nursing, Midwifery and Allied Health Professions.

In addition, the National electronic Library for Health (NeLH),[56] a Government gateway that provides details of various databases on guidelines, links to health know-how, healthcare knowledge and health management, can be accessed. A virtual branch library of the NeLH has been proposed which will be dedicated to the health of older people.

Another organisation in this field that might act as a portal to links is the British Society of Gerontology (BSG),[57] which provides a section on gerontology resources on the Web.

Patient information and patient advocacy

Part of the Government's initiative to involve and keep the public informed, as well as offering health advice, has resulted in the 24-hour telephone call service NHS Direct, as well as a gateway to health information on the Internet.[58] It is an easy-to-use site with a special category for the concerns of older people, which is found listed under '64+'. Contained in this section, for example, are details of the recent *National Service Framework for Older People*, reports published by various health organisations, tips on how to care for yourself, and details of Care Direct, a new 24-hour telephone helpline aimed specifically at older people, which is currently being piloted.

Another patient information gateway is Patient UK,[59] which is a directory of websites that provide information on health, disease and illness. It is sponsored by a commercial organisation and edited by two GPs. It has a section on 'Seniors' Health' that gives comprehensive coverage of Internet sites of relevance to the concerns of the older person.

Both Age Concern[60] and Help the Aged[61] provide factsheets on aspects of health. For example, Age Concern has recently published a document entitled *Help With Continence* (May 2001), and Help the Aged has an 'Info Point' section in which it lists its own self-help sheets.

Quality improvement

The Clinical Effectiveness Evaluation Unit of the Royal College of Physicians has published the findings of a national sentinel clinical audit of evidence-based prescribing for older people.[62] Help the Aged's *Dignity on the Wards*[63] campaign highlighted concerns about the treatment of older people in hospital. The Clinical Resource Audit Group in Scotland has funded a three-year audit of the nutrition of elderly people living in long-term care. The site publishes an executive summary and a full report of the findings.[64]

The British Geriatrics Society (BGS) in partnership with the Royal College of Physicians[65] has published guidelines for the implementation of clinical governance in geriatric medicine. These are available from the BGS site. The document looks at the manpower commitment and resources required to undertake clinical governance within the acute setting. The two organisations also offer a list of primary topics 'of key relevance to the specialty'. These include management of falls, stroke, delirium, dementia and depression, continence problems, Parkinson's and other syndromes, pressure sores, resuscitation issues, rehabilitation after fractured femur and evidence-based prescribing.

Box 4.2 Regional NHS modernisation programmes for older people

Northern and Yorkshire Region[66] have constructed a detailed site describing their implementation of plans to meet the priorities of the National Service Frameworks and NHS plan. The area for 'Older People' holds improving practice articles, indicators of performance and news updates.

Improving practice articles include action on prevention of falls, approaches for preventing strokes, and descriptions of a Community Resource Team for older people and a Rapid Response Team for older people with mental health problems in crisis. Indicators of performance include graphs of delayed discharges as a percentage of people aged 75 years and over occupying a hospital bed by health authority, and emergency readmission rates for patients aged 75 years and over (for those readmitted within 7 and 28 days).

The South-West regional office publishes a compendium of intermediate care and other initiatives aimed at redesigning services for older people.

The *Our Healthier Nation in Practice* database[67] offers numerous descriptions of projects aimed at improving healthcare delivery or aspects of health promotion for older people. The *NHS Beacons* programme[68] is also part of the modernisation agency, and publishes information about projects with a view to disseminating good practice. Currently the site offers records on Beacons addressing older people and mental health services.

Box 4.3 Finding resources about the care of older people with dementia

Suppose that you are beginning an information-gathering exercise about the care of older people with dementia. At this point it might be too early to articulate a particular research question using the PICO mnemonic (*see* page 17). Nevertheless, you want to cast a net into the deep waters of the World Wide Web. Where do you begin? It is important to have some structure within which to work. The chapters in this book which are dedicated to areas of care are organised in a way that can help to plot out an information-gathering exercise such as this one. Organise your search around five themes, namely evidence-based practice, health policy, gateways, patient information and quality improvement. Do not forget offline resources such as bibliographic databases available on CD from libraries.

Evidence-based practice covers secondary sources such as guidelines and systematic reviews, as well as tacit knowledge. The Scottish Intercollegiate Guidelines Network (SIGN) published a clinical guideline on *Interventions in the Management of Behavioural and Psychological Aspects of Dementia*[69] in 1998.

Systematic reviews and critically appraised topics. Check the Cochrane Library,[20] *Clinical Evidence*[26] and the Centre for Reviews and Dissemination.[22] *Bandolier*[27] has grouped its commentaries on published research. These include several on dementia, one of which highlights the difficulties surrounding accurate diagnosis and effective treatment.

Primary research. Certain research centres have published reports on aspects of dementia care. The National Primary Care Research and Development Centre published a report on *Older Carers of Frail Older People and the Interfaces with Primary Care Services* in 2001.[70] The *BMJ* has gathered together articles on dementia published since January 1998.[71]

Health policy. The National Service Framework for Older People[1] includes eight standards including guidance on the integration of mental health services to improve diagnosis, treatment and support. An earlier important report from the Audit Commission is *Forget Me Not: Mental Health Services for Older People.*[72]

Gateways. The Dementia Research Group and CANDID (Counselling and Diagnosis in Dementia) maintain a site called *Dementia Web*,[73] based at the National Hospital for Neurology and Neurosurgery. The Social Science Information Gateway (SOSIG),[38] OMNI[54] and NMAP[55] also provide online databases of evaluated sites.

Patient information and patient advocacy. emental-health.com,[74] Mind[75] and Patient UK[59] are just some of the sites offering fact sheets describing dementia. The Alzheimer's Society[76] provides advice and fact sheets, a review of quality research in dementia and campaigns for better services. The Society, while welcoming the NSF, commented on the lack of detail and practical standards for dementia care.

Quality improvement. The Royal College of Nursing in partnership with Help the Aged have published an informative online resource about acute hospital care and older people with dementia and acute confusion.[77] Other sources of important case studies and examples of good practice include OHN,[67] Health Action Zones[78] and Beacon sites.[68]

References

1   http://www.doh.gov.uk/nsf/olderpeople.htm

2   http://www.shef.ac.uk/misc/groups/bgshsrsi/Icconfreport.htm

Secondary sources of evidence

Evidence-based clinical practice guidelines

3   http://www.nice.org.uk/

4   http://www.nice.org.uk/nice-web/Article.asp?a=247&ss=guidelines

5   http://www.rcn.org.uk/services/promote/clinical/clinical_guidelines.htm

6   http://www.rcgp.org.uk

7   http://www.nice.org.uk/catlist.asp?c=20116

8   http://www.show.scot.nhs.uk/sign/home.htm

9   http://www.rcplondon.ac.uk/college/ceeu/ceeu_guidelinesdb.asp

10 http://www.nelh.nhs.uk/

11 http://www.eguidelines.co.uk

12 http://www.bmj.com/cgi/content/full/321/7267/1007?view=full&pmid=11039974

13 http://www.bapen.org.uk/

14 http://www.stroke.org.uk/rcp1pr.htm

15 http://www.n-i.nhs.uk/crest/

16 http://www.rcgp.org.uk

17 http://www.ncl.ac.uk/chsr/publicn/tools/dmentg26.htm
18 http://www.resus.org/uk/pages/guide.htm
19 http://www.guidelines.gov

Systematic reviews and critically appraised topics

20 http://www.update-software.com/clibhome/clib.htm
21 http://www.cochrane.org/cochrane/orgs.htm
22 http://www.york.ac.uk/inst/crd
23 http://www.hebw.umcm.ac.uk
24 http://www.hebw.uwcm.ac.uk/injury/chapter2.html
25 http:// cebm.jr2.ox.ac.uk/cats/catsearch.html
26 http://www.clinicalevidence.org.uk
27 http://www.jr2.ox.ac.uk/bandolier/
28 http://www.bham.ac.uk/arif/elderlyhealth.htm
29 http://www.bgs.org.uk/compendium/

Primary sources of evidence

30 http://www.ncb.nlm.nih/gov/PubMed
31 http://www.bmj.com/all.shtml
32 http://enb.org.uk
33 http://www.update-software.com/National/nrr-product.html
34 http://www.doh.gov.uk/research/rd3/information/findings.htm
35 http://www.cpa.org.uk/
36 http://www.kcl.ac.uk/kis/schools/life_sciences/health/gerontology/
37 http://www.liv.ac.uk/HumanAgeing/
38 http://www.sosig.ac.uk/roads/subject-listing/World-cat/older.html

Tacit knowledge

39 http://www.jiscmail.ac.uk/lists/agenet.html
40 http://www.jiscmail.ac.uk/lists/bgs-training.html

41 http://www.bgs.org.uk/trainindex.htm

42 http://www.doh.gov.uk/ntrd/chain/chain.htm

Policy in the four countries

43 http://www.nhs.uk/nationalplan/summary.htm

44 http://www.doh.gov.uk/nsf/olderpeople.htm

45 http://www.doh.gov.uk/ncsc/carehomes.pdf

46 http://www.doh.gov.uk/essenceofcare/intro.htm

47 http://www.doh.gov.uk/continenceservices.htm

48 http://www.n-i.nhs.uk/crest/

49 http://www.show.scot.nhs.uk/

50 http://www.show.scot.nhs.uk/shas/Reports/OP%20Assessment%20Framework.
pdf

51 http://www.researchweb.org.uk/ncsc/olderpeoplepreface.htm

52 http://www.assembly.wales.gov.uk/healthplanonline/

53 http://www.wales-nhs.uk/

Gateways

54 http://omni.ac.uk

55 http://nmap.ac.uk/

56 http://www.nelh.nhs.uk/

57 http://www.soc.surrey.ac.uk/bsg/

Patient information and patient advocacy

58 http://www.nhsdirect.nhs.uk/main.jhtml

59 http://www.patient.co.uk

60 http://www.ageconcern.org.uk/

61 http://www.helptheaged.org.uk

Quality improvement

62 http://www.rcplondon.ac.uk/college/ceeu_ebop_home.htm

63 http://www.helptheaged.org.uk

64 http://www.show.scot.nhs.uk/crag/topics/nutrition/

65 http://www.nyx.org.uk/modernprogrammes/olderpeople/

66 http://www.doh.uk/swro/olderpeopleservices.htm

67 http://www.ohn.gov.uk/database/database.htm

68 http://www.nhsbeacons.org.uk/

Finding resources about care of older people with dementia

69 http://www.show.scot.nhs.uk/sign/

70 http://www.npcrdc.man.ac.uk/

71 http://www.bmj.com/cgi/collection/dementia

72 http://www.audit-commission.gov.uk/publications/brmhsop.shtml

73 http://dementia.ion.ucl.ac.uk/

74 http://www.emental-health.com/

75 http://www.mind.org.uk/

76 http://www.alzheimers.org.uk

77 http://www.rcn.org.uk/dementia/

78 http://www.haznet.org.uk/

5

Mental health

Paula Lavis

Mental health is a vast subject. Depending on your definition, it can include promotion and maintenance of good mental health, management of specific mental health problems, and mental health service development. This makes the potential scope for information absolutely vast. This chapter will mainly deal with adult mental health, but will also mention items that are particularly relevant to children, young people and older people.

Mental health problems cover a broad spectrum of conditions that vary in their severity and persistence. Some are recognised as a psychiatric disorder (i.e. they are recognised by an established classification system such as ICD-10[1] or DSM-IV),[2] whilst other mental health problems seem to be an assortment of different behavioural and emotional problems. In addition, there are other factors such as co-morbidity and dual diagnosis (mental health problems and either substance misuse or learning disability).

Secondary sources of evidence

Evidence-based clinical practice guidelines

Clinical guidelines and systematic reviews tend to focus on conditions at the severe end of the spectrum, perhaps because of their severity and/or their persistence. Moreover, as is mentioned in Chapter 6 on child health, there are very few guidelines specifically aimed at young people.

The Scottish Intercollegiate Guidelines Network (SIGN)[3] has published guidelines on psychosocial interventions in schizophrenia,[4] interventions in the management and behaviour and psychological aspects of dementia,[5] and attention deficit hyperkinetic disorders in children and young people.[6]

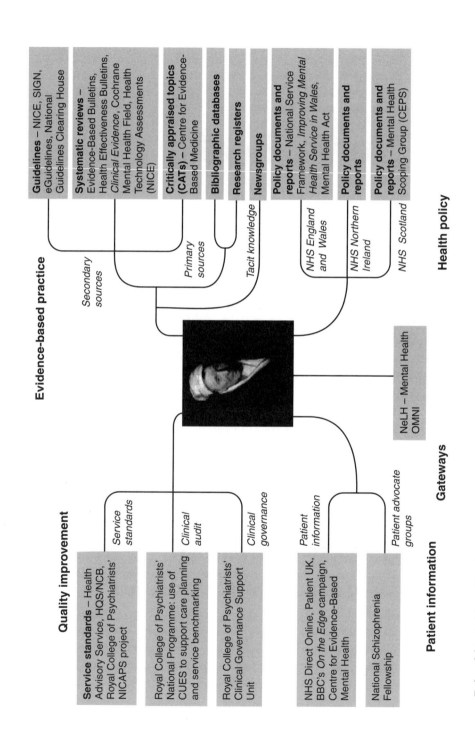

Evidence-based practice

Guidelines – NICE, SIGN, eGuidelines, National Guidelines Clearing House

Systematic reviews – Evidence-Based Bulletins, Health Effectiveness Bulletins, *Clinical Evidence*, Cochrane Mental Health Field, Health Technology Assessments (NICE)

Critically appraised topics (CATs) – Centre for Evidence-Based Medicine

Bibliographic databases

Research registers

Newsgroups

Secondary sources

Primary sources

Tacit knowledge

Health policy

Policy documents and reports – National Service Framework, *Improving Mental Health Service in Wales*, Mental Health Act

Policy documents and reports

Policy documents and reports – Mental Health Scoping Group (CEPS)

NHS England and Wales

NHS Northern Ireland

NHS Scotland

Gateways

NeLH – Mental Health OMNI

Quality improvement

Service standards – Health Advisory Service, HQS/NCB, Royal College of Psychiatrists' NICAPS project

Royal College of Psychiatrists' National Programme: use of CUES to support care planning and service benchmarking

Royal College of Psychiatrists' Clinical Governance Support Unit

Service standards

Clinical audit

Clinical governance

Patient information

NHS Direct Online, Patient UK, BBC's *On the Edge* campaign, Centre for Evidence-Based Mental Health

National Schizophrenia Fellowship

Patient information

Patient advocate groups

Figure 5.1 Mental health site map.

SIGN has several other mental health topics covered by their development programme,[7] including postnatal depression and anxiety disorders.

Clinical practice guidelines have been developed by the British Psychological Society's Centre for Outcomes Research and Effectiveness (CORE)[8] and the Royal College of Psychiatrists' Research Unit[9] (CRU). CORE has published a guideline on the effectiveness of psychological therapies and counselling,[10] while CRU has published a guideline on the management of imminent violence.[11]

Both of these organisations will jointly manage the National Collaborating Centre for Mental Health that will lead on the development of mental health guidelines commissioned by NICE.[12] Their programme of work is initiated by the Secretary of State for Health and the National Assembly for Wales, based on national priorities. The first three mental health guidelines, which will be developed in a rolling programme, will be on schizophrenia, depression and eating disorders. They will be followed by guidelines on self-harm, management of disturbed behaviour in inpatient psychiatric settings, and drug treatments and psychological therapies for anxiety and related disorders. You can find details of the guideline development programme at the NICE website.

The eGuidelines[13] website is produced by the Medendium Publishing Group Ltd, and provides access to summaries of guidelines which are relevant to primary care, and to *Practice Guidelines*, their monthly journal. Access to the website is free of charge once one has registered. Both of the publications mentioned above are published as hard copy as well.

The National Guidelines Clearing House (NGC)[14] is a database of evidence-based guidelines. It is based in the USA, and is run by the Agency for Healthcare Research and Quality[15] (AHRQ). The criteria for inclusion of guidelines are that they are evidence based, written in English and published since 1995. You can either run a search using keywords, or you can browse the NGC by various means. At present, the only options in the Disease/Condition category are Diseases or Mental Disorders. However, a considerable number of guidelines are captured here, including those developed by the American Psychiatric Association[16] and the American Academy of Child and Adolescent Psychiatry.[17]

Systematic reviews

The Cochrane Library[18] database contains several systematic reviews on the subject of mental health. If you search using the MeSH (Medical Subject Heading) term 'Mental Disorders', you will find a number of systematic reviews.

The Cochrane Collaboration has a few specialist groups, who are responsible for the creation and updating of Cochrane's systematic reviews. Most of the groups have their own website, but you can also obtain information from the Cochrane Library database. Group websites give information about who is in the group, what they are involved in, and where you can contact them.

The Cochrane Depression, Anxiety and Neurosis Group[19] is concerned with the evaluation of healthcare relevant to mood disorders, anxiety disorders, somatoform disorders, chronic fatigue syndrome, dissociative disorders and eating disorders, as well as clinically significant problems such as deliberate self-harm and suicide attempt.

The Cochrane Schizophrenia Group[20] is concerned with the evaluation of the prevention and treatment of non-affective, functional, psychotic illness and the rehabilitation of patients with this condition. There is also the Developmental, Psychosocial and Learning Problems Group, which addresses a range of medical, social, educational and socio-legal problems. Unfortunately it does not have a website, but you can obtain some information about the group from the Cochrane Collaboration's website.[21]

Effective Health Care Bulletins are based on systematic reviews and produced bimonthly by the NHS Centre for Reviews and Dissemination.[22] The website puts up a warning if you try to access some of the older bulletins – this is because they state that their bulletins are likely to be valid for about one year. However, they do give suggestions as to where you can look for more up to date information.

The bulletins which are available online and that are relevant to mental health are as follows:

- *Mental Health Promotion in High-Risk Groups*[23]
- *Deliberate Self-Harm*[24]
- *Drug Treatments for Schizophrenia*[25]
- *Psychosocial Interventions for Schizophrenia.*[26]

The NHS Centre for Reviews and Dissemination produces other reports, and this website gives an A–Z list of their publications.[27] These include brief bulletins called *Effectiveness Matters*, which have covered counselling in primary care as a topic.[28] They also produce CRD Reports, which discuss the results of systematic reviews, but in more depth than Effective Health Care Bulletins. These are not free of charge, but there is generally an online version of the executive summary. There are several of these on the topic of forensic mental health.[29]

Clinical Evidence[30] is a compendium of evidence, and is available either as a publication or online via the Internet. However, it is available by subscription only, unless you work in the NHS. If you are in the latter category, you can obtain free access via the National electronic Library for Health (NeLH).[31] Once your status as an employee of an NHS organisation has been verified, you will be issued with an Athens password. Consult the website for further information.[32] *Clinical Evidence* contains a section on mental health covering Alzheimer's disease, anxiety disorders, bulimia nervosa, depressive disorders, depressive disorders in children and adolescents, obsessive-compulsive disorder, post-traumatic stress disorder and schizophrenia.

There is a separate section on poisoning, and this currently includes paracetamol poisoning. It is worth noting that factors which are often associated with a mental health problem, such as poisoning or self-harm, are often placed in a separate category.

The Royal College of General Practitioners' Clinical Practice Evaluation Programme (CPEP) has produced *Evidence-Based Aspects of Care* and *Review Criteria for the Primary Care Management of Adults with Depression*.[33] An index to the *Aspects of Care* series is available online.[34] This document is derived from recommendations from the available evidence-based guidelines. The CPEP describe the *Aspects of Care* series as 'a starting point for local educational activities and to set local standards of care'. They also state that the local review criteria can be used for clinical audit.

Health Evidence Bulletin – Wales[35] collates the best current evidence for a variety of subject areas. The section on mental health has collated evidence on personality disorder, delirium, dementia, eating disorder, bipolar disorder, major depression, schizophrenia, anxiety and suicide.

Turning Research into Practice (TRIP)[36] contains links to evidence-based resources. They have recently developed an 'Extended Area' which covers specific specialist areas, one of which is mental health.[37] These areas contain all of the recent additions to the database which fall within the subject category. It is also colour coded, so it is easy to identify the different types of evidence.

The publication *Bandolier* has organised its content online to include certain specialist subsites, one of which is mental health. The articles cover a range of themes, but each takes as its point of departure a review[38] of trial evidence, and provides a critical summary of the findings.

Primary research

The National Research Register[39] of research commissioned by the Department of Health is available online. It is a database of completed and ongoing research commissioned by or of interest to the NHS. Each entry generally gives information about the name of the project, contact details for the lead researcher, a summary of the project, and the date when it is due to be completed.

The Research Findings electronic Register (ReFeR)[40] gives access to the findings of completed research from the NHS Research and Development

Programme. Again this database provides access to information about the nature of the research, who is doing it, and a summary of the research findings.

The national NHS Research and Development Programme has recently changed from a relatively large number of time-limited programmes to three programmes,[41] namely Health Technology Assessment (HTA), Service Delivery and Organisation (SDO) and New and Emerging Technologies (NEAT). However, you might find some useful research projects among the NHS Executive Research Programmes. These will be phased out as the research projects come to an end. The following programmes might be of interest to mental health workers:

- Mother and Child Health R&D Programme[42]
- National Mental Health Programme[43]
- Forensic Mental Health Research and Development[44] – this website provides links to the programme's current and completed research.

There is a link on the above website to the Virtual Institute of Severe Personality Disorder.[45] This institute brings together 11 academic units conducting research in this field, and provides a vehicle for networking.

The Home Office's Research and Development and Statistics Directorate website provides access to various reports,[46] including research covering the interface between mental health services and the justice system. For instance, one can gain access to the report on *National Evaluation of the Youth Offending Teams.*[47]

The website of National Statistics (previously called the Office of National Statistics) contains details of various research projects conducted in the field of mental health.[48] For instance, you can access the summary to the national survey on the prevalence of child and adolescent mental health problems.[49]

The Audit Commission has been involved in various national research projects, such as their report on mental health services for older people.[50] They have also published information about child and adolescent mental health services (CAMHS).[51]

Research units and research networks

It is beyond the scope of this chapter to provide more than a brief overview of the type of information that is available from centres undertaking research in the field of mental health. Described below are some of the units that are actively publishing and disseminating research findings together with research support networks.

One example of such a unit is the Centre for Suicide Research,[52] based at Oxford University. Their website gives information on current and published research, as well as providing links to statistical information.

The Thomas Coram Research Unit[53] is based within the Institute of Education. It is a designated research unit of the Department of Health, and the focus of its research is on children and young people both within and outside their families. Much of the unit's research which could be described as falling within a mental health remit is generally in the field of mental health promotion. However, they have recently been involved in a research project on adolescent self-harm, the aim of which was to develop national policy and guidance on how to manage young people who present at Accident and Emergency departments with self-harming behaviours.

The Royal College of Psychiatrists' Research Unit (CRU)[9] is involved in various research projects and quality initiatives. CRU has also established the FOCUS[54] group, which is involved in child and adolescent mental health. There is online access to several of their publications and an email discussion group.[55]

The Sainsbury Centre[56] aims to improve mental health services by influencing national policy and practice through a programme of research, service development and training.

Tacit knowledge

Mailing lists are very effective ways of accessing tacit knowledge, since they provide an opportunity for you to pick people's brains about a shared interest. However, mailing lists are only useful if they are active – that is, if people are contributing rather than just 'lurking', reading emails posted to the list but never actively contributing to it. Most mailing lists are hosted by a parent organisation. There is wide variation in the service that one can expect. Most lists seem to be free of charge to join, but there are a few which are subscription only.

Mailbase[57] provides a service over and above merely allowing you to send and receive emails. For instance, you can search the lists archive and you can search across mailing lists. JISCmail[58] has superseded Mailbase, but certain lists are still available from it, such as the Royal College of Psychiatrists Clinical Governance mailing list.[59]

JISCmail hosts a large number of mailing lists of interest to the research community. For instance, it hosts the Psychiatric Nurses mailing list.[60] If you cannot find a list for your particular interest, you can start your own. However, you will have to meet JISC's criteria.

The Network for Psychiatric Nursing Research is a membership-funded network for disseminating and developing research and practice development in the UK. It is connected to the Royal College of Nursing's Mental Health Programme.[61]

Policy in the four countries

Mental health has been a priority area since *The Health of the Nation*[62] set health targets across a range of conditions. There has been a flow of initiatives from the Labour Government dealing with or impacting on mental health services. In addition, there are policy documents from other Government departments which impact on mental health services, such as the Social Exclusion Unit's reports[63] and the Child and Young People's Unit,[64] from the Department of Education and Employment.

The National Service Framework for Mental Health[65] addresses the mental health needs of working-age adults up to 65 years. It sets out national standards, national services models and local action and programmes for implementation. A National Service Framework for Older People[66] includes mental health needs (*see* Chapter 4), as does that planned for children[67] (*see* Chapter 6).

Documents that look at practical ways in which the National Service Framework (NSF) can be operationalised include *A Practical Guide to the National Service Framework for Mental Health*[68] from the Primary Care Research and Development Unit, the *Mental Health Implementation Guide* from the Department of Health[69] and *Making it Happen*, produced by the mental health promotion organisation Mentality.[70] The report is about implementing Standard One of the NSF.

Mental health is one of the core national health priorities at the heart of the NHS Plan.[71] The latter sets out a radical strategy taking in primary care support for GPs, early intervention in psychosis, crisis resolution teams, assertive outreach services, services for women, support for carers, and high secure hospital and prison services. Mental health is a priority area within the *Our Healthier Nation*[72] site. You can search the database for initiatives which aim to deliver on the mental health targets.

The Mental Health Act (1993) is undergoing an extensive review in order to create a new legislative framework that reflects modern patterns of care and treatment for severe mental illness. You can read the White Paper *Reforming the Mental Health Act*[73] and the Commons Select Committee Reports[74] which monitor the Government's progress against its agenda for reform.

The Mental Health Information Strategy[75] describes the way in which the Government's plans for information management and technology, *Information for Health*, will be implemented in order to achieve 'modern mental healthcare delivery'.

The strategy for modernising mental health services in Wales, for both child and adolescent mental health services[76] and adult mental health services, is available online.[77]

Scottish Health on the Web has published both the strategy document, *A Framework for Mental Health*,[78] and a wider plan for modernising the NHS in Scotland, *Our National Health: a Plan for Action, a Plan for Change*.[79] The Mental Health Act is also under review.[80] The Scottish Health Advisory Service (SHAS) has published quality indicators for mental health,[81] and these will underpin its role as an inspectorate, evaluating and advising mental health services in Scotland. The Clinical Standards Board has published clinical standards for schizophrenia.[82]

Gateways

The two most important mental health gateways in the UK are the Centre for Evidence-Based Mental Health[83] and the National electronic Library for Mental Health[84] (*see* Box 5.1).

Box 5.1 Centre for Evidence-Based Mental Health and National electronic Library for Mental Health

The Centre for Evidence-Based Mental Health (CEBMH) promotes and supports the teaching and practice of evidence-based mental healthcare. It works closely with other organisations such as the Royal College of Psychiatrists and NHS Direct Online. Its websites provide links to various online publications, including guidelines, online journals and educational materials.

The CEBMH is the host organisation for the National electronic Library for Mental Health (NeLMH), a virtual branch library of the National electronic Library for Health (NeLH). The Centre works in association with NHS Direct and the National electronic Library for Mental Health to produce theme months giving patient information on specific conditions. So far there have been theme months devoted to depression and schizophrenia.[85]

---

emental-health.com[86] is a not-for-profit project created by Zeus, a company that specialises in communications about mental health. The website was launched in February 2001 and provides information, news and discussion relevant to schizophrenia and related psychoses, Alzheimer's disease and other dementias, depression and bipolar disorder. You need to register online with the site in order to gain access to all of the features of the site (e.g. the discussion lists).

The Mental Health Foundation has a portal for mental health and learning disabilities information called Connects.[87] It also requires registration before all of its features can be accessed.

Patient information and patient advocacy

A MORI[88] poll in February 2001 revealed that around 60% of people who used the Internet would use it to seek help for mental health problems. They valued the convenience but also the anonymity of the medium. The report confirmed an earlier survey conducted by MORI on behalf of the British Medical Association which found that this did not reflect dissatisfaction with consultations with GPs. Worryingly, only 9% of the 2073 people who were interviewed believed that the information they were accessing might be unreliable.

Clearly there is a great appetite for patient-focused information.

One of the fascinating aspects of the influence of Internet communications is how reputable information providers are finding innovative ways to engage the public. We have already mentioned the work of the partnership between NHS Direct Online, the Centre for Evidence-Based Mental Health and the National electronic Library for Mental Health. A deliberately narrow sample of information providers is described below.

The Royal College of Psychiatrists has posted its patient information on a web page.[89] There is a wide variety of information for all age groups, and a range of different conditions are covered. The College also runs campaigns that might be of interest to a broader audience than just healthcare professionals.[90]

The BBC is another high-profile organisation with a growing interest in developing health information sites online. It has a mental health section[91] that provides general information on different conditions, and contact details for help and advice, as well as information on support groups. The BBC has also run several campaigns, such as *On the Edge*,[92] a guide to emotional well-being.

The emental-health[86] site is also designed to provide information about a range of mental health problems. The site has been developed in conjunction with the Royal College of Psychiatrists' *Changing Minds: Every Family in the Land* campaign.

The Patient UK[93] site contains a specific section on mental health self-help and support groups. You can also search the site for other patient information by condition.

YoungMinds[94] is a charity that publishes information booklets for young people and their parents or carers on various mental health issues. It publishes a range of information leaflets in PDF format, such as *What is Attention Deficit Disorder?* Adobe Acrobat (free software) is required in order to read these.

The National Schizophrenia Fellowship[95] is one of the largest charities devoted to severe mental illness. It provides patient information on schizophrenia and medication, and they have also designed a subsite aimed specifically at young adults – the @ease[96] site. This area is particularly impressive in the way that it makes use of the attractiveness of the medium to the young, and it would be of particular value as a resource for a wider audience interested in reflecting on mental health issues.

Mind[97] has produced a range of information booklets, samples of which are available online. One series, called *Understanding...*, gives accessible and clear explanations on a range of mental health issues. Mind also publishes a series of *How to...*[98] booklets aimed at mental health improvement. Mind's website has a number of other features, including a section on Government policy, with Mind's own commentary (e.g. on the reform of the Mental Health Act) and a summary of the Mind inquiry into social exclusion, *Creating Accepting Communities*.

Box 5.2 NHS Direct Online theme months

NHS Direct in association with the Centre for Evidence-Based Mental Health (CEBMH) has produced two websites which focus on specific mental health problems. The first of these was on depression, and the most recent one is on schizophrenia. The sites contain useful information about the nature of the condition, how it is treated, etc., as well as a list of further reading and contact details of support groups.

These sites are developed with the help of input from various sources. For instance, the CEBMH has a discussion group, and they ask members of the list to suggest sources for the further reading and support group section. They then collate all of this information and test it out on the members of the mailing list and other stakeholders before the site goes live.

This connects with the NeLMH, which aims to pool together information on mental health for professionals and members of the public alike.

The Mental Health Foundation[99] divides its work into three areas:

1 the mental health of children and young people (e.g. the Brighter Futures work looks at targets for three groups, aged 5–12, 12–16 and 16–21 years, respectively)
2 the mental health of working adults (e.g. alternatives to hospital treatment and SPIRAL – systemic prevention, recovery and learning)
3 mental health in later life (e.g. dementia home care).

The World Health Organization[100] selected mental health to be the focus of its World Health Day for 2001. Its aim was to heighten awareness about mental health, including the concern that at least one in every four people who turn to the health services for help is troubled by disorders which are often not diagnosed, and therefore not treated.

Another campaigning site, affiliated to the Sainsbury Centre for Mental Health, is the Mentality site.[101] It is geared to promoting mental health and helping health authorities to meet NSF targets, and it also publishes tips for those considering developing and publishing their own material.

Quality improvement

Service standards and benchmarking

The Royal College of Psychiatrists' Research Unit (CRU) has been actively and systematically collecting information on carers' and users' expectations of services[102] (CUES). These experiences are being collected from community mental health services, and the project aims to support individual care planning and service benchmarking. The CRU website provides some general information about their quality network for inpatient child and adolescent mental health services. The membership is run on a subscription basis, so access to further documentation is restricted.

The NHS Beacons initiative[103] contains information on mental health services that are willing to share good practice. Each Beacon service has applied to the NHS Modernisation Agency and agreed to participate in a range of dissemination activities, from workshops to CD-ROMs and interactive learning days. You will find Beacon sites listed under mental health (primary and forensic), personality disorders, CAMHS services and mental health services for older people.

The Sainsbury Centre has a database of mental health services called the Practice Database,[56] which is searchable by service type, type of organisation or locality. Each record contains information on who the service is for, and why it is (or is not) a model of good practice. The Sainsbury Centre also published (in April 2001) standards for primary care organisations commissioning mental health services, and developed competences for clinicians implementing the NSF for mental health, called *The Capable Practitioner*.[56] Other initiatives to develop benchmarks for mental health services can be found at the Inner Cities Mental Health Group site[104] and the UK Quality Indicators Project.[105]

The Government has funded projects with the aim of developing innovative ways of delivering services in child and adolescent mental health. The projects needed to be multidisciplinary and required both local and overarching evaluation. More information is available from the YoungMinds website.[106]

Clinical audit

The Royal College of Psychiatrists' National Inpatient Child and Adolescent Psychiatry Study (NICAPS)[107] was commissioned by the Department of Health. Its aims are to identify child and adolescent inpatient units in England and Wales. It also details the quality of services provided by a sample of these units, and in addition includes a longitudinal study of the outcomes of referrals to these units.

The National Confidential Inquiry into Suicide and Homicide by People with Mental Illness[108] was established at the University of Manchester in 1996. Data were collected from 1996 to 2000, and the report based on the findings was published in 2001. You can access further details of the aims, methodology and key findings of the report from the website.

Box 5.3 Looking for evidence with regard to alternatives to inpatient provision for people with mental health problems

There has been a big move towards looking for alternatives to inpatient provision, but suppose that you feel that you want to assess the available evidence with regard to these alternatives and inpatient care to help you to decide what the model(s) of care should be in your area.

This is a five-step process. The stages are as follows.

1 Ask a focused question.
2 Search for the best evidence.
3 Critically appraise it (i.e. decide whether it is any good for your purposes).
4 Implement it.
5 Audit it, or use some form of quality assurance.

You can use the PICO mnemonic to tease out the elements of the problem.

P defines the patient or problem (e.g. people with complex and severe mental health problems).
I defines the issue being considered (e.g. alternatives to inpatient provision).
C gives a comparison (e.g. assertive outreach, psychosocial education).
O describes the clinical outcome of interest (e.g. less likely to relapse, mental health status improves, etc.).

This is quite a complex search because the alternatives could be numerous, so it is probably best to brainstorm for suggested alternatives and then prioritise those interventions for which you will search for evidence.

So these are the key elements of our search. Now we need to look at the different forms of evidence (secondary, primary and tacit forms) to address the problem:

- secondary evidence – guidelines, systematic reviews
- primary evidence – original research
- tacit knowledge – discussion groups around this area.

Working through this framework we might consider reviewing the following:

- Effective Health Care Bulletin on Psychosocial Interventions for Schizophrenia[26]
- Cochrane Collaboration – various systematic reviews of the evidence with regard to alternatives[18]
- Government policy: National Service Framework,[65] Assertive Outreach in the NHS Plan[71]
- National Research Register[39] and ReFeR database[40]
- online journals for primary research (e.g. *British Journal of Psychiatry, Psychiatric Bulletin*, etc.).

Discussion groups: various, including Psychiatric Nursing JISCmail list.[60]

References

1 World Health Organization (1992) *Tenth Revision of the International Statistical Classification of Diseases and Related Health Problems*. World Health Organization, Geneva; http://www.who.int/whosis/icd10/

2 American Psychiatric Association (2000) *Diagnostic and Statistical Manual of Mental Disorders* (4e). Text revision. American Psychiatric Association, Washington, DC.

Secondary sources of evidence

Evidence-based clinical practice guidelines

3 http://www.sign.ac.uk

4 http://www.sign.ac.uk/pdf/sign30.pdf

5 http://www.sign.ac.uk/pdf/sign22.pdf

6 http://www.sign.ac.uk/guidelines/fulltext/52/index.html

7 http://www.sign.ac.uk/guidelines/development/index.html

8   http://www.doh.gov.uk/mentalhealth/treatmentguide/index.htm

9   http://www.rcpsych.ac.uk/cru/index.htm

10 http://www.psychol.ucl.ac.uk/CORE/glines.html

11 http://www.rcpsych.ac.uk/publications/guidelines/index.htm

12 http://www.nice.org.uk

13 http://www.eguidelines.co.uk/

14 http://www.guidelines.gov/index.asp

15 http://ahrq.gov/

16 http://www.psych.org/clin_res/prac_guide.cfm

17 http://www.aacap.org/clinical/parameters.htm

Systematic reviews

18 http://www.update-software.com/clibhome/clib.htm

19 http://www.ccdan.auckland.ac.nz/

20 http://cebmh.warne.ox.ac.uk/csg/

21 http://www.cochrane.org/cochrane/contact.htm

22 http://www.york.ac.uk/inst/crd/ehcb.htm

23 http://www.york.ac.uk/inst/crd/ehc33.htm

24 http://www.york.ac.uk/inst/crd/ehc46.htm

25 http://www.york.ac.uk/inst/crd/ehc56.htm

26 http://www.york.ac.uk/inst/crd/ehc63.htm

27 http://www.york.ac.uk/inst/crd/publicats.htm

28 http://www.york.ac.uk/inst/crd/em52.htm

29 http://www.york.ac.uk/inst/crd/crdrep.htm

30 http://www.clinicalevidence.org/

31 http://www.nelh.nhs.uk

32 http://www.nelh.nhs.uk/home_use.asp

33 http://www.shef.ac.uk/~scharr/publich/cpep/AdultDep.pdf

34 http://www.shef.ac.uk/~scharr/publich/cpep/ebrc.html

35 http://hebw.uwcm.ac.uk/mental/index.html

36 http://www.tripdatabase.com

37 http://www.tripdatabase.com/ea/mh/1.htm

38 http://www.jr2.ox.ac.uk/bandolier/

Primary research

39 http://www.update-software.com/nrr/CLIBINET.EXE?A=1&U=
    1001&P=10001
40 http://www.doh.gov.uk/research/rd3/information/findings.htm
41 http://www.doh.gov.uk/research/rd3/national.htm
42 http://www.doh.gov.uk/research/mch/index.htm
43 http://www.doh.gov.uk/nth&york/nmhp.htm
44 http://www.doh.gov.uk/fmhrd.htm
45 http://www.doh.gov.uk/hspscb/visped.htm
46 http://www.homeoffice.gov.uk/rds/index.htm
47 http://www.homeoffice.gov.uk/rds/pdfs/occ69-newstrat.pdf
48 http://www.statistics.gov.uk
49 http://www.statistics.gov.uk/pdfdir/mhc0300.pdf
50 http://www.audit-commission.gov.uk/ac2/NR/Health/brmhsop.htm
51 http://www.audit-commission.gov.uk/ac2/NR/Health/brcamhs.htm

Research units and research networks

52 http://cebmh.warne.ox.ac.uk/csr/
53 http://www.ioe.ac.uk/tcru/default.htm
54 http://www.rcpsych.ac.uk/cru/focus/index.htm
55 http://www.mailbase.ac.uk/lists/focus
56 http://www.scmhonline.org.uk/

Tacit knowledge

57 http://www.mailbase.ac.uk/lists/
58 http://www.jiscmail.ac.uk
59 http://www.mailbase.ac.uk/lists/cgss/
60 http://www.jiscmail.ac.uk/lists/psychiatric-nursing.html
61 http://www.man.ac.uk/rcn/ukwide/npnr.html

Policy in the four countries

62 Department of Health (1991) *The Health of the Nation: a consultative document for health in England*. HMSO, London.

63 http://www.socialexclusionunit.gov.uk/

64 http://dfee.gov.uk/cypu/home_what.shtml

65 http://www.doh.gov.uk/nsf/mentalhealth.htm

66 http://www.doh.gov.uk/nsf/olderpeople.htm

67 http://www.doh.gov.uk/nsf/children.htm

68 http://www.npcrdc.man.ac.uk/Pages/Publications/PDF/mh-hbk.pdf

69 http://www.doh.gov.uk/mentalhealth/implementationguide.htm

70 http://www.doh.gov.uk/mentalhealth/makingithappen.htm

71 http://www.nhs.uk/nhsplan

72 http://www.ohn.gov.uk/database/database.htm

73 http://www.doh.gov.uk/menhlth.htm

74 http://www.publications.parliament.uk/pa/cm199899/cmselect/cmhealth/

75 http://www.doh.gov.uk/nhsexipu/strategy/nsf/2.htm

76 http://www.wales.gov.uk/subihealth/content/pdf/men-health-e.pdf

77 http://www.wales.gov.uk/subihealth/content/pdf/adult-health-e.pdf

78 http://www.show.scot.nhs.uk/publications/mental_health_services/

79 http://www.show.scot.nhs.uk/sehd/onh/onh-00.htm

80 http://www.scotland.gov.uk/millan

81 http://www.show.scot.nhs.uk/shas/Other%20Pages/publications.htm

82 http://www.clinicalstandards.org/home.asp

Gateways

83 http://www.cebmh.com/

84 http://www.nelmh.org/

85 http://www.psychiatry.ox.ac.uk/cebmh/elmh/schizophrenia/

86 http://www.emental-health.com/

87 http://195.13.121.137/mhf/portal/index.htm

Patient information and patient advocacy

88 http://www.mori.com/polls/2001/zeus.shtml

89 http://www.rcpsych.ac.uk/info/index.htm

90 http://www.rcpsych.ac.uk/campaigns/index.htm

91 http://www.bbc.co.uk/health/mental/

92 http://www.bbc.co.uk/health/ote/index.shtml

93 http://www.patient.co.uk/selfhelp/mental.htm

94 http://www.youngminds.org.uk

95 http://www.nsf.org.uk/

96 http://www.at-ease.nsf.org.uk/

97 http://www.mind.org.uk/

98 http://www.mind.org.uk/information/information_understanding.asp

99 http://www.mentalhealth.org.uk

100 http://www.who.int/world-health-day/index.en.html

101 http://www.mentality.org.uk/

Quality improvement

Service standards and benchmarking

102 http://www.rcpsych.ac.uk/cru/auditcues.htm

103 http://www.nhsbeacons.org.uk

104 http://freespace.virgin.net/j.way/

105 http://www.ncl.ac.uk/Psychiatric_indicators.htm

106 http://www.youngminds.org.uk/mhg.html

Clinical audit

107 http://www.rcpsych.ac.uk/cru/hsrp/nicaps.htm

108 http://www.confidentialinquiry.man.ac.uk/

6

Child health

Clinicians caring for children need to be aware of the evidence about the benefits and harms of preventive manoeuvres, diagnostic strategies, treatments and rehabilitation techniques. Child health researchers need motivation and funding to do more research to generate data to guide clinical decisions. The researchers, clinicians and other decision makers (e.g. administrators and government officials) also need to communicate more effectively to ensure the transfer of research into clinical practice that does more good than harm to children. We have no excuse for not practising evidence-based paediatrics. We have no excuse for not getting more and better evidence.[1]

Secondary sources of evidence

Evidence-based clinical practice guidelines

Child health is not well served by evidence-based clinical practice guidelines developed in the UK. Only a few of the publications from the Scottish Intercollegiate Guidelines Network[2] relate to paediatrics and child health. However, all of this may change now that the National Institute for Clinical Excellence[3] has established six guideline development and audit units called Collaborating Centres. One of these is dedicated to the production of guidelines in the field of Women and Child Health.

Another source of information about clinical practice guidelines is the eGuideline database[4] produced by Medendium, which focuses on guidelines in primary care. You need to register online to gain access to summaries of guidelines. Other sections of the site are only available to paying subscribers.

The most important repository of guidelines outside the UK is the National Guidelines Clearing House (NGC).[5] The NGC is sponsored by the Agency for Healthcare Research and Quality[6] (formerly the Agency for Health Care Policy and Research) in partnership with the American Medical Association and the American Association of Health Plans.

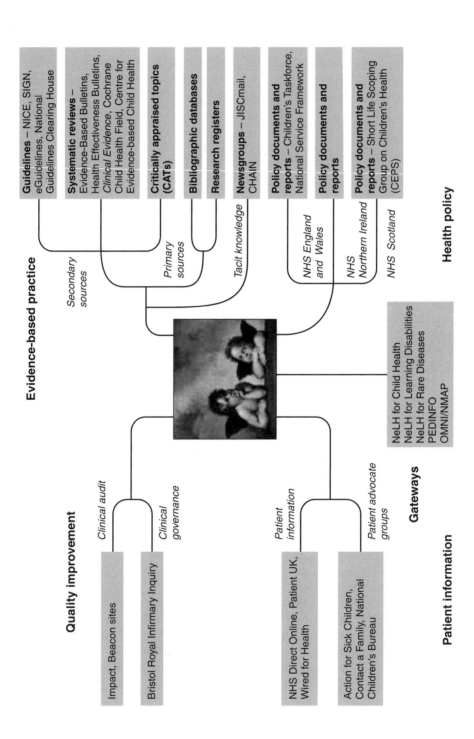

Evidence-based practice

Secondary sources

Guidelines – NICE, SIGN, eGuidelines, National Guidelines Clearing House

Systematic reviews – Evidence-Based Bulletins, Health Effectiveness Bulletins, *Clinical Evidence*, Cochrane Child Health Field, Centre for Evidence-based Child Health

Critically appraised topics (CATs)

Primary sources

Bibliographic databases

Research registers

Tacit knowledge

Newsgroups – JISCmail, CHAIN

NHS England and Wales

Policy documents and reports – Children's Taskforce, National Service Framework

NHS Northern Ireland

Policy documents and reports

NHS Scotland

Policy documents and reports – Short Life Scoping Group on Children's Health (CEPS)

Health policy

Quality improvement

Clinical audit

Impact, Beacon sites

Clinical governance

Bristol Royal Infirmary Inquiry

Patient information

NHS Direct Online, Patient UK, Wired for Health

Patient advocate groups

Action for Sick Children, Contact a Family, National Children's Bureau

Patient information

Gateways

NeLH for Child Health
NeLH for Learning Disabilities
NeLH for Rare Diseases
PEDINFO
OMNI/NMAP

Figure 6.1 Child health site map.

Systematic reviews

Fortunately the situation is healthier with regard to systematic reviews. The Cochrane Collaboration has formed a Child Health Field.[7] The Cochrane Collaboration is an international organisation that enables people to prepare, maintain and promote the accessibility of systematic reviews of the effects of healthcare interventions. Reviews are updated as new research emerges, and are held on an electronic database called the Cochrane Library[8] (*see* Chapter 2), which provides fast and easy access to research information. Since its inception in 1998, the Child Health Field has focused on synthesising evidence on conditions that affect children (age 0–18 years). The Cochrane Library currently contains more than 100 systematic reviews concerning health problems in children. Cochrane reviews are updated regularly, and new reviews are added with each issue, so it is important to search the most recent issue.

The following sites are all based within the UK and should be regularly monitored for news of developments in the field of child health.

The NHS Centre for Reviews and Dissemination (CRD)[9] based at the University of York has published a well-established series of syntheses of research on clinical effectiveness, cost-effectiveness and acceptability of health service interventions, called *Effective Health Care Bulletins*.[10] Most of the recent series are available online. Bulletins of interest to clinicians who are caring for children cover prevention and reduction of the adverse effects of unintended teenage pregnancies,[11] preschool hearing, speech, language and vision screening,[12] deliberate self-harm,[13] prevention of the uptake of smoking in young people,[14] and prevention of unintentional injuries in children and young adolescents.[15] The CRD has also published a report on the effectiveness of interventions used in the treatment/management of chronic fatigue syndrome and myalgic encephalomyelitis (ME) in adults and children.[16]

Health Evidence Bulletins – Wales is a collaborative project involving health authorities, providers of primary and secondary healthcare, and library and information units. So far they have published systematic reviews for maternal and early child health and learning disabilities. All of the reviews are available in full text from http://hebw.uwcm.ac.uk/.[17]

The Royal College of Paediatrics and Child Health is also publishing summarised guides to published studies called CHERUBs (*see* Royal College of Paediatrics and Child Health website). Further systematic reviews can be found in academic units such as the Evidence-Based Child Health Unit, Department of Child Health, University of Liverpool[18] and the Centre for Evidence-Based Child Health – Institute of Child Health, London.[19]

The Turning Research Into Practice (TRIP) database[20] was created in 1997. It contains links to 'evidence-based' resources in that the publishers all applied explicit critical appraisal techniques to the research literature. It has since developed an 'extended area' of about a dozen specialist areas, including child health. Here you can quickly access digests of evidence

---

Box 6.1 Clinical Evidence – Child Health

Clinical Evidence is a compendium of reviews of available evidence on a range of common clinical interventions, covering medical, surgical, nursing and complementary fields. It is published by the BMJ Publishing Group.[21] The contents are updated and expanded twice a year, so there should be no concerns about the currency of the evidence.

It is a tribute to the quality of the publication that the Department of Health and the Scottish Health Executive have negotiated the central purchase of *Clinical Evidence* for NHS staff. Access to the electronic version will be available to NHS staff through NHS Net[22] and the National electronic Library for Health.[23]

Clinical Evidence exploits the way in which the World Wide Web can 'add value' to a publication. Subscribers to it can access an online version by using their customer number as a password. The website is being used to gather comments from subscribers and suggestions for new topics. Subscribers can access updates as they come online without waiting for the printed copy.

The technology is also working in other ways. The Web version is being hyperlinked to the National Library of Medicine PubMed[24] database (*see* Chapter 2). This means that PubMed users can follow links to further information from *Clinical Evidence*, including full text versions of certain sections.

As infodetectives we need to be acutely aware of the provenance of the evidence that is supplied in publications such as these. *Clinical Evidence* is at pains to make its quality assurance and review development methods explicit.[21]

Each area follows a distinctive format. A condition is defined together with its incidence/prevalence, aetiology and risk factors, prognosis, aims of interventions and outcomes. Questions are then framed on the effects of treatments and the preventive interventions.

For instance, in the Child Health section, the item on acute otitis media asks 'What are the effects of treatments?' and then cycles through the effects of treatment options (analgesia, antibiotics, shorter vs. longer courses of antibiotics), describing the benefits and harmful effects and commenting on them. The same format is adhered to for preventive interventions.

Each condition is prefaced by the key messages from the evidence.

Clinical Evidence provides a detailed commentary on the thinking behind the design and presentation of research findings, as well as a glossary explaining the terms that are frequently used in the text.

such as systematic and clinical reviews, as well as guidelines and original studies appearing in peer-reviewed journals.

Critically appraised topics and numbers needed to treat

One of the intriguing ways in which the World Wide Web is influencing clinical decision making is by finding novel ways of developing and updating the knowledge base. Critically appraised topics (CATs) are one method. They are a means of articulating and answering clinical questions about diagnosis and interventions. They set out to appraise the evidence for its validity (closeness to the truth) and applicability (usefulness in our clinical practices). You can find out more about them from the Centre for Evidence-Based Medicine (CEBM) at the University of Oxford.[25] The CEBM has its own CAT bank – a database of critically appraised topics that is searchable and available free of charge from their website.[26]

The CEBM has links to other CAT banks, including online databases in other centres featuring child-health-related CATs, namely the University of Michigan,[27] the University of North Carolina,[28] the University of Rochester[29] and the University of Washington.[30]

Although there are few child-related CATs in the CEBM CAT bank, another feature of their site is a collection of numbers needed to treat (NNTs).[31] This is a measure of the effect of a treatment. 'It is the number of people you would need to treat with a specific intervention for a given period of time to prevent one additional adverse outcome or achieve one beneficial outcome' (*Clinical Evidence*). Here you can find figures for the effectiveness of several interventions relating to children, such as otitis media prevention and asthma management.

Primary sources of evidence

For an overview of developments within the Department of Health's Research and Development programme, visit the Department's own research area.[32]

You can search for completed and ongoing research projects commissioned by the NHS from the National Research Register.[33]

You can keep track of current research priorities by using the Research Findings electronic Register[34] (ReFeR) site from the Department of Health. Here you can monitor the progress of time-limited national Research and Development programmes such as the one for Mother and Child Health.[35] The site provides details of each priority area and links these to the commissioned studies.

Tacit knowledge

The Internet is enabling people to link up and exchange information in many different ways. Still the most powerful means of answering questions posed by peers or others who share a common interest is through discussion groups or lists.

JISCmail[36] hosts lists for the higher education community in the UK. Here you can review lists that are relevant to paediatrics and child health. For example, you can review messages to the paediatric nursing forum which was created in 1998 to enable children's nurses and other healthcare professionals to have an arena in whch to 'share ideas, knowledge and expertise'.

For a discussion of how email discussion lists work and some useful lists in the area of evidence-based practice, visit the website of the School of Health and Related Research at the University of Sheffield.[37] The examples given include the Cochrane Collaboration's Child Health field list.[38]

CHAIN (Contacts, Help, Advice and Information Network) is a network that brings together healthcare professionals, librarians, teachers and researchers who are interested in evidence-based practice. Details of how to join the network are available from the CHAIN website.[39]

Policy in the four countries

The National Service Frameworks[40] are one of the forces used by the Department of Health to drive up service standards within the NHS. Fortunately, child health services have a National Service Framework[41] and a Children's Taskforce to push ahead with aspects of the NHS Plan relating to children.[42]

In Scotland, the Clinical Resources and Audit Group has established a time-limited project to establish a number of child-health-related clinical effectiveness projects. You can read a report describing the method used to prioritise topics and develop the programme portfolio.[43] Other bodies that provide important insight into child health services include the Audit Commission,[44] which has published reports on child and adolescent mental health services[45] (*Children in Mind*) and children in hospital[46] (*Getting the Best Out of Children's Services*).

Gateways

Gateways or portals provide a convenient way of finding subject-specific information in one place. However, they can vary considerably in how well they are structured and maintained.

In the UK, OMNI[47] and its sister gateway NMAP[48] should provide access to evaluated websites relating to paediatrics and child health. The records have been submitted by information specialists from professional bodies and libraries, and have been subjected to published evaluation criteria. You can browse the terms used to index records in order to establish the extent of collections in your area of interest.

One of the longest-standing paediatric gateways is PEDINFO, subtitled 'an Index of the Pediatric Internet'. It is maintained by the University of Alabama.[49]

Box 6.2 National electronic Library for Health and its child health content: National electronic Library for Child Health, National electronic Library for Learning Disabilities and National electronic Library for Rare Diseases

We have already discussed the aims and ambitions of the National electronic Library for Health (NeLH). Fortunately for this area of healthcare, there are several NeLH projects of interest. Plans are well advanced for a National electronic Library for Child Health,[50] but this will be only one of three Virtual Branch Libraries. Libraries for Rare Diseases and Learning Disabilities have also been proposed.

The basis for the National electronic Library for Child Health is the PIER[51] site. This site has been developed with the support of Sheffield Children's Hospital NHS Trust, the Royal College of Paediatrics and Child Health and an educational grant from Merck Sharp and Dohme. The intention is to keep running costs low, and although the site requires registration, access remains free.

The site contains various sections. The guidelines area includes locally developed guidelines from organisations such as acute hospitals (e.g. a guideline developed for children with epilepsy by the Royal Liverpool Children's Hospital). The criteria for inclusion are that the guidelines are evidence based and make the links between recommendations and the knowledge base explicit. The multi-media area contains images, X-rays and video clips. A review section contains both specially commissioned articles and links to online journal articles. Unfortunately, this means that certain articles are only available to members of the Royal College of Paediatrics and Child Health. The review section will expand to contain clinical problem pages that cover issues seldom referred to in textbooks. The site will also host discussion groups and develop specialist areas such as one for specialist registrars. The patient information and links to self-help groups contain information that has not been peer reviewed. However, the site is compiling a comprehensive and searchable resource.

Patient information and patient advocacy

The Internet has created an explosion of information designed for and by patients and their carers. Children's charities have been quick to take advantage of the medium. Perhaps this was in recognition of the fact that families themselves were attracted to Internet communications, as they provided access to information and a means of exchanging information with each other.

Websites aimed at children and their carers display increasing sophistication and creativity. The Captain Chemo[52] site from the Royal Marsden Hospital is based on a cartoon character drawn by a patient. There are two adventures to follow which focus on the side-effects of treatment for childhood cancers. The @ease site[53] from the National Schizophrenia Fellowship also displays information graphically. This site is aimed at mental health issues and young people.

Contact a Family[54] is the only UK charity that provides support and advice to parents whatever the medical condition of their child. They have collated information on over 1000 rare syndromes and rare disorders, and can put families in touch with each other through their *Directory of Specific Conditions and Rare Disorders*. The information in the Directory forms part of the service provided by NHS Direct Online[55] (*see* Chapter 2).

Patient UK[56] is a directory of UK websites that provide information on health, disease and illness. It is edited by two GPs and is sponsored by Norwich Union Healthcare. The Directory covers the broad spectrum of health and has a section on child health.

Action for Sick Children[57] and the National Children's Bureau[58] both focus on the interests of children and young people. Action for Sick Children's website contains information for health professionals as well as parents and carers. For example, the site has a number of free information sheets, including one on helping children to cope with pain.

The National Children's Bureau website has a feature, written in partnership with Research in Practice,[59] of monthly research and policy updates. These are intended to assist managers and team leaders in child and family service agencies. However, they will be helpful to anyone interested in keeping up to date with national research and policy developments.

Box 6.3 Wired for Health

Wired for Health[60] is a collaboration between the Department of Health and the Department of Education and Employment to 'ensure that young people and their teachers are able to access relevant and appropriate information at the touch of a button' (*Our Healthier Nation: A Contract for Health*, February 1998).

Content is developed around a range of audiences.

Key Stage 1 (4–7 years) resource is called Welltown.

Key Stage 2 (7–11 years) resource is called Galaxy H. Both Key Stage 1 and 2 sites cover areas of personal, social and health education (PSHE) and citizenship set out in the National Curriculum.

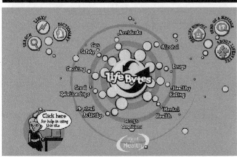

Key Stage 3 (11–14 years) resource is called LifeBytes. LifeBytes aims to provide this age group with relevant and appropriate health information, as well as linking to a range of evaluated websites on the health issues that it covers.

Key Stage 4 (14–16 years) resource is called Mind, Body and Soul. This site gives information about accidents, alcohol, drugs, healthy eating, mental health, physical activity, sexual health, smoking and sun safety.

Quality improvement

It is one thing to identify the evidence for the effectiveness or otherwise of interventions in healthcare, but it is quite another to change or influence your own practice or that of others involved in the delivery of care. Not so long ago, finding models from real-life projects in the NHS was difficult. However, the World Wide Web has helped to disseminate much-needed advice and experience from units that have tackled quality improvement projects.

The NHS Beacons programme[61] is one such initiative and we cover this more fully in Chapter 5 on mental health and Chapter 4 on care of the elderly. Another much-needed source of information is ImpAct,[62] a sister publication to the evidence-based review *Bandolier*. Back numbers of ImpAct are searchable from the *Bandolier* website. A quick search of this resource uncovered a description of how a team from Sutton in Surrey tackled the problem of integrating services for children with special needs.

The investigation into events at the Bristol Royal Infirmary[63] represented a watershed in public attitudes towards the medical establishment. It provided a focus for demands for greater accountability within the NHS, and it strengthened the Government's resolve to implement a system which would ensure that this could happen.

The inquiry triggered a detailed examination of many issues, including patient communication of clinical risk, clinical competencies, whistle-blowing, the actual extent of iatrogenic illness in the UK, and the need for interdisciplinary training. The official website published the proceedings of the inquiry, and the final report makes many recommendations that have major implications for the health service.

One strand of the report dealt with safeguarding patient safety and the challenge of developing a system for monitoring adverse events. The National Patient Safety Agency[64] has been established to implement just such a system, and its website will provide some insight into whether the NHS is being transformed from a 'club' culture into a learning organisation.

Box 6.4 Pain: using the World Wide Web as a resource for practice development

Suppose that you are a nurse working on an acute paediatric ward. You are concerned that many of the children do not get adequate pain relief postoperatively. The ward does not have a formal method of pain assessment. How would you find out what are the most effective methods of pain assessment?

Let us first use the PICO mnemonic to tease out the elements of the problem.

P defines the patient or problem being addressed (e.g. children recovering from surgery)
I defines the 'thing' being considered (e.g. methods of pain assessment)
C gives a comparison (e.g. various methods of pain assessment)
O describes the clinical outcome of interest (e.g. early recognition and assessment of pain).

From here we can assemble the key elements of our search. We can use the different types of evidence (secondary, primary and tacit forms) to address the problem. As discussed earlier, we can characterise the knowledge base as consisting of the following:

• secondary evidence in the form of guidelines or systematic reviews
• primary evidence in the form of original research
• tacit knowledge in the form of discussion groups related to paediatric pain management.

A quick appraisal of these reveals that there has been a guideline on the recognition and assessment of children's pain from the Royal College of Nursing.[65] You may also consider sources of systematic reviews such as the Cochrane Library,[8] since it has an active Child Health field.[7] Another site that aims to bring together systematic reviews with pain as an outcome is the Oxford Pain Internet Site.[66] This site contains a number of systematic reviews featuring pain management in children.

There are many specialist research centres and projects related to this topic. The Foundation of Nursing Studies[67] has posted details of its project to promote standards for paediatric pain assessment. The Pediatric Pain Sourcebook[68] is hosted by the IWK Grace Health Centre and the Psychology Department, Dalhousie University, Canada. It includes guidelines, research, policies and patient information relating to paediatric pain.

You might also check discussion groups with a focus on this theme, such as the Pediatric Pain Discussion List[69] (run by the same team as the Pediatric Pain Sourcebook), which is an international Internet forum for informal discussion of any topic related to pain in children. Recurrent themes of the list include clinical problems or questions, research problems or proposals, announcements of meetings, book reviews, and political or administrative aspects of children's pain management and prevention. You might find yourself becoming an active participant!

Remember that the process consists of five steps. Identifying and searching for the best evidence are steps 1 and 2. Critically appraising, applying and then evaluating your practice are the remainder. Support for appraisal of your performance might be available in the form of implementation tools (*see* the Royal College of Nursing website for information about implementing the pain guideline[70]).

References

1 Feldman W (1998) Evidence-based paediatrics. *Evidence-Based Med.* **5**: 134–5; http://www.library.utoronto.ca/medicine/ebm/syllabi/child/intro.htm

Secondary sources of evidence

Evidence-based clinical practice guidelines

2 http://www.show.scot.nhs.uk/sign/home.htm

3 http://www.nice.org.uk

4 http://www.eguidelines.co.uk

5 http://www.guidelines.gov/

6 http://www.ahrq.gov/

Systematic reviews

7 http://www.cochranechildhealth.org/

8 http://www.update-software.com/clibhome/clib.htm

9 http://www.york.ac.uk/inst/crd/

10 http://www.york.ac.uk/inst/crd/ehcb.htm

11 http://www.york.ac.uk/inst/crd/ehc31warn.htm

12 http://www.york.ac.uk/inst/crd/ehc42warn.htm

13 http://www.york.ac.uk/inst/crd/ehc46warn.htm

14 http://www.york.ac.uk/inst/crd/ehc55warn.htm

15 http://www.york.ac.uk/inst/crd/ehc25warn.htm

16 http://www.york.ac.uk/inst/crd/cfs.htm

17 http://hebw.uwcm.ac.uk/

18 http://www.liv.ac.uk/childhealth/ebchu.htm

19 http://www.ich.bpmf.ac.uk/ebm/ebm.htm

20 http://www.tripdatabase.com/

21 http://www.clinicalevidence.org

22 http://www.doh.gov.uk/research/whatsnew.htm

23 http://www.nelh.nhs.uk/home_use.asp

24 http://www.ncb.nlm.nih/gov/PubMed

Critically appraised topics and numbers needed to treat

25 http://cebm.jr2.ox.ac.uk/docs/cats/catabout.html

26 http://cebm.jr2.ox.ac.uk/docs/catbank.html

27 http://www.ped.med.umich.edu/ebm/cat.htm

28 http://www.med.unc.edu/medicine/edursrc/!catlist.htm

29 http://www.urmc.rochester.edu/MEDICINE/RES/CATS/index.html

30 http://depts.washington.edu/pedebm/

31 http://cebm.jr2.ox.ac.uk/nnts/allnnts.html

Primary sources of evidence

32 http://www.doh.gov.uk/research/

33 http://www.update-software.com/National/

34 http://www.doh.gov.uk/research/

35 http://www.doh.gov.uk/research/mch/priority/index.htm

Tacit knowledge

36 http://www.jiscmail.ac.uk/

37 http://www.shef.ac.uk/~scharr/ir/email.html

38 http://www.cochrane.org/chlist.html

39 http://www.doh.gov.uk/ntrd/chain/faqs.htm

Policy in the four countries

40 http://www.doh.gov.uk/nsf/nsfhome.htm

41 http://www.doh.gov.uk/nsf/children.htm

42 http://www.doh.gov.uk/qualityprotects/info/publications/ taskforce.pdf

43 http://www.show.scot.nhs.uk/crag/committees/ceps/childrpt.htm

44 http://www.audit-commission.gov.uk/

45 http://www.audit-commission.gov.uk/acz/Nk/Health/brcamhs.htm

46 http://www.audit-commission.gov.uk/publications/nrchildserv.shtml

Gateways

47 http://omni.ac.uk/

48 http://nmap.ac.uk/

49 http://www.pedinfo.org/

50 http://www.nelh.shef.ac.uk/nelh/

51 http://www.pier.shef.ac.uk/

Patient information and patient advocacy

52 http://www.royalmarsden.org/captchemo/index.asp

53 http://www.at-ease.nsf.org.uk/

54 http://www.cafamily.org.uk/

55 http://www.nhsdirect.nhs.uk/main.html

56 http://www.patient.co.uk/child_health.htm

57 http://www.actionforsickchildren.org/index2.html

58 http://www.ncb.org.uk/

59   http://www.rip.org.uk
60   http://www.wiredforhealth.gov.uk/

Quality improvement

61   http://www.nhsbeacons.org.uk/
62   http://www.jr2.ox.ac.uk/bandolier/
63   http://www.bristol-inquiry.org.uk
64   http://www.npsa.org.uk/

Pain

65   http://www.rcn.org.uk/professional/CPG Contents.pdf
66   http://www.jr2.ox.ac.uk/bandolier/booth/painpag/
67   http://www.fons.org/
68   http://is.dal.ca/~painsrc/
69   http://neurosurgery.mgh.harvard.edu/pedipain.htm
70   http://www.rcn.org.uk/professional/CPG Pain Assessment 1-20.pdf

7

Primary care

The NHS Plan[1] has given primary care a leading role in the modernisation of the health service. Central to the plan is the development of primary care trusts – new entities designed to control the budget for improving the health of and delivering healthcare to communities of about 100 000 people. The strategy is designed to empower general practitioners working with other health professionals and NHS managers. They will have responsibilities to implement local plans and national policies.

Whatever the look of primary care in the future, certain trends are obvious. The 'greying' population and a substantial increase in minor consultations will have implications for the flexibility of primary healthcare teams and the nursing workforce in particular. Yet the improvements sought by the Government through clinical governance activities will impact upon all members of the primary care team. Developing an awareness of the range of resources available online will be an important step in acquiring the additional knowledge necessary to meet the challenge.

Secondary sources of evidence

Evidence-based clinical practice guidelines

Clinical guidelines relevant to primary care can be found on the NICE[2] and SIGN[3] websites. However, the eGuidelines[4] site is devoted to guidelines developed for the primary care sector. The site is intended for healthcare professionals and requires the completion of an online registration form. Members of the public are directed to a sister website, healthnetUK.[5] Registered users can search a database of guideline summaries across a range of subject areas. The guideline summaries are updated three times a

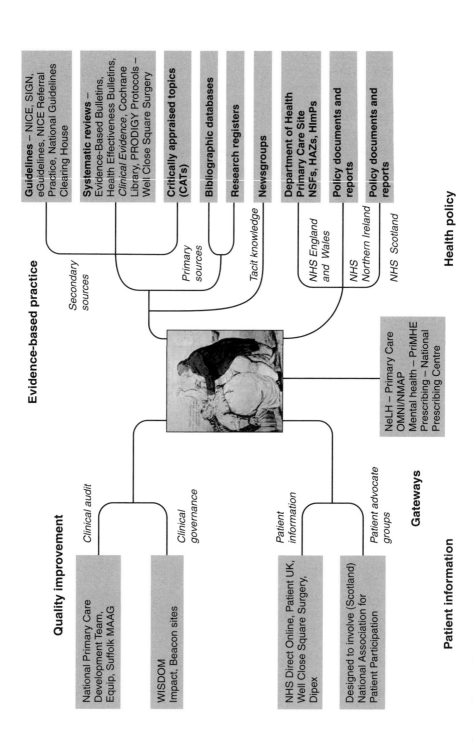

Evidence-based practice

Guidelines – NICE, SIGN, eGuidelines, NICE Referral Practice, National Guidelines Clearing House

Systematic reviews – Evidence-Based Bulletins, Health Effectiveness Bulletins, *Clinical Evidence*, Cochrane Library, PRODIGY Protocols – Well Close Square Surgery

Critically appraised topics (CATs)

Bibliographic databases

Research registers

Newsgroups

Secondary sources

Primary sources

Tacit knowledge

Health policy

Department of Health Primary Care Site NSFs, HAZs, HImPs

Policy documents and reports

Policy documents and reports

NHS England and Wales

NHS Northern Ireland

NHS Scotland

NeLH – Primary Care OMNI/NMAP Mental health – PriMHE Prescribing – National Prescribing Centre

Gateways

Quality improvement

Clinical audit

Clinical governance

National Primary Care Development Team, Equip, Suffolk MAAG

WISDOM Impact, Beacon sites

Patient information

Patient advocate groups

NHS Direct Online, Patient UK, Well Close Square Surgery, Dipex

Designed to involve (Scotland) National Association for Patient Participation

Patient information

Figure 7.1 Primary care site map.

year, and each one is colour coded to denote a particular type of guidance (e.g. dark blue indicates a NICE guideline) or a particular status (e.g. those recommended by the NHS Executive are light blue).

Systematic reviews and critically appraised topics

The Cochrane Library[6] and the NHS Centre for Reviews and Dissemination[7] at the University of York provide details of systematic reviews some of which will be pertinent to primary care. It is worth noting that the National electronic Library for Primary Care[8] offers what it calls a 'meta-evidence' search of Cochrane, *Bandolier*,[9] the Centre for Evidence-Based Medicine,[10] the National Institute for Clinical Excellence and *Effectiveness Matters*.[11]

The evidence base from the Health Development Agency[12] is still in the early stages of development, but looks set to be a significant resource for public health. The searchable database contains systematic reviews of effectiveness, literature reviews, meta-analyses, expert group reports and other review-level information 'about what works to improve health and reduce health inequalities'. The site of the Health Education Board for Scotland[13] performs the same function.

Protocols

Many general practices will develop their own protocols around commonly occurring conditions. The Well Close Square Surgery in Berwick-on-Tweed[14] has devised a website displaying these (*see* Box 7.1).

Box 7.1 Well Close Square Surgery

The Well Close Square Surgery is one of a select but growing number of practices with an extremely well-developed Web presence. This award-winning site is of special interest because of the way it makes available information for patients and material such as the care protocols underpinning care delivery.

Both the patient information and care protocol sections are well structured and easily accessible. The Patient Information Leaflets (PILs) have been written by members of the practice.

The care protocols are organised according to a branching structure, from high-level labels (e.g. 'cardiovascular') to the next subsidiary level (e.g. 'anaphylaxis' to 'weight loss'). The cardiovascular section has a special area devoted to the National Service Framework for Coronary Heart Disease.

The 'doctor' area of the site includes resources for clinical governance activities such as audit and performance review, in addition to GP and nurse training.

Primary sources

A number of academic units and research centres are disseminating details of their work online. The King's Fund[15] has a rich section on primary care, and has published information on studies relating to type 2 diabetes, care of older people and walk-in centres, among others.

The Centre for Innovation in Primary Care (CIPC) is an NHS-funded charity based in Sheffield.[16] It has been undertaking studies aimed at sharing good practice since 1990. Current themes include overviews of initiatives designed to reduce demand for hospital services, and improving patient access to general practice.

The Unit for Evidence-Based Practice and Policy[17] describes itself as a 'virtual subunit' of the Department of Primary Care and Population Sciences at University College London. It has published information about its research programme, including a randomised controlled trial of evidence-based outreach education for GPs focusing on ways of influencing prescribing decisions (the EBOR project), and a qualitative study looking at the theory–practice gap in evidence-based primary care called 'Life's too short and the evidence too hard to find'.

The National Research Register of research commissioned by the Department of Health[18] is available online. It is a database of completed and ongoing research commissioned by or of interest to the NHS. Each entry generally gives information on the name of the project, contact details for

---

Box 7.2 National Primary Care Research and Development Centre

The National Primary Care Research and Development Centre (NPCRDC) is based at the University of Manchester.[19] The website gives details of the following projects run by the Centre.

- National Tracker Survey[20] – the aim of this survey is to establish how primary care groups and trusts are managing their core functions of health improvement, developing primary and community services and commissioning hospital services.
- General Practice Assessment Survey (GPAS)[21] – this survey asks for patient views about general practice. The software for undertaking and analysing patient surveys was developed by the NPCRDC. GPAS is not to be confused with GPASS (a primary care system used in Scotland).
- National Database for Primary Care Groups and Trusts[22] – this contains details of socio-economic and demographic characteristics, together with indicators of general health status for all primary care groups and primary care trusts in England.

the lead researcher, a summary of the project, and the date when it is due to be completed.

Tacit knowledge

Internet discussion groups provide much-needed forums for the exchange of experience and information. Lists on the JISCmail service include the following.

- GP-UK[23] – this list facilitates discussion of new ideas, research, work-shops, seminars, conferences, grants, education, software development, etc., for the UK general practice (family medicine) community. Non-UK views are also welcome. GP-UK intends to promote collaborative work, problem solving and support.
- HEALTH PROMOTION[24] – people working in the field of health pro-motion can use this list to discuss topics of interest to their profession. It was set up in the Trent region of the UK.
- PRIMSTAT[25] – this is a forum for the exchange of expertise in areas of medical statistics that are particularly relevant to primary care by statisticians who are involved in or interested in primary care research.
- HAZ-EVALUATION[26] – the aim of this list is to bring together indi-viduals who are interested in evaluation and learning from the Health Action Zone (HAZ) initiative in England and Northern Ireland. The list will include researchers who are participating in the evaluation of local and national HAZ initiatives.
- NETLIST[27] – this list is open to anyone involved in the co-ordination or administration of a primary care research network in the UK. Its pur-pose is to help networks to share information.

Policy in the four countries

The Department of Health Primary Care[28] section provides detailed information on a broad range of initiatives, including clinical governance (*see* section on quality improvement below), structure and administration (e.g. GP fees and initiatives such as NHS primary care walk-in centres) and actions to tackle rough sleeping.

For NHS Scotland the easiest route to information about current policy is via the Scottish Health on the Web (SHOW)[29] site. The Information and Statistics Division[30] is a subsite of SHOW and has a large report library relating to therapeutics and other epidemiological data in its primary care section. There is a 'Scot GP'[31] discussion forum among those hosted by the SHOW site.

Beyond SHOW the Clinical Standards Board for Scotland[32] (CSBS) has a Primary Care Reference Group and in March 2000 published a report of quality initiatives within practice-based primary care across Scotland. The CSBS site contains national clinical standards relating to cancer, coronary care and mental health. In Scotland the initiative to engage public involvement in primary care planning has spawned its own site called 'Designed to Involve'.[33]

The Welsh equivalent of SHOW is the Health of Wales Information Service (HOWIS).[34] Primary Care Wales is the Welsh primary care website,[35] where you can find *Improving Health in Wales. The Future of Primary Care: a Consultation Document* (published in July 2001).

Gateways

Because primary care is such a diffuse subject area, there is a pressing need for gateways and subject specialist portals. We have already mentioned the National electronic Library for Primary Care[8] (NeLH-PC). However, there are many others – each with its own particular take on primary care.

Box 7.3 National electronic Library for Primary Care

The National electronic Library for Primary Care is one of the Virtual Branch Libraries of the National electronic Library. The site attempts to provide an overview of primary care concerns, and it organises content into a 'knowledge' area and a 'know-how' area.

The knowledge area consists of the following subsections: references, journals, books, therapeutics, emergency, news and business, technology, education, and research and papers.

'Know-how' features evidence-based medicine tools, an A to Z of guidelines, policy, project management and governance areas. Clinical subject areas such as diabetes, cancer and National Service Frameworks are included here. The EBM search tool provides what the site calls a 'meta-evidence search' of the Cochrane Library, *Bandolier*, Evidence-Based Medicine, the National Institute for Clinical Excellence and *Effectiveness Matters*.

The third 'view' offered by the site is a professional one providing links relevant to members of the primary healthcare team, such as nurses and allied health professions.

Primary care report,[36] ukpractice™,[37] Clinnix professional,[38] the National Association of Primary Care[39] and NHS Alliance[40] operate within this sector. For example, ukpractice™ is available on free registration to all accredited UK medical professionals. It aims to fulfil the need for 'a single community offering up-to-the-minute information and education'. Through its partners and affiliations, ukpractice™ offers courses aimed at GPs and nurses and searchable databases such as a vaccinations guide and a 'cross-referenced diseases testing and treatment database'.

Not surprisingly, there are a number of sites developing around primary care subspecialties. For example, PriMHE[41] is a charity dedicated to primary care mental health education. Another area that is challenging primary care is the upsurge in minor illnesses, so it is notable that there is a Minor Illness website.[42]

Box 7.4 Prescribing online

A GP prescribes in the region of 250–350 items per week, making it the 'most common therapeutic approach taken when treating patients in the NHS'.[43] A GP writing in *He@lth Information on the Internet,*[44] although grateful that there were a number of excellent sites available in this area, hoped that one day there might be a convenient method for drawing these together either by means of a single supersite or via a meta-search engine. Until this happens, users are in the unenviable position of integrating the fragments themselves. Fortunately, on-line prescribing is a rich area, and it is worth making the effort to become familiar with what is on offer.

The *British National Formulary* is available online as the eBNF.[45] It does not require registration – a fact that should not be lost on the public or the primary care team that wishes to promote better understanding and active self-management. *MIMS* (the *Monthly Index of Medical Specialties*) is available online, too,[46] but this requires registration and evidence that one is a health professional. Both of these sites can be found in the therapeutics section of the NeLH-PC.

The National Prescribing Centre[47] was founded in 1996 by the Department of Health 'to facilitate the promotion of high-quality, cost-effective prescribing through a co-ordinated and prioritised programme of activities aimed at supporting all relevant professionals and senior managers working in the modern NHS'. The site publishes nurse prescribing guidance and Medicines Resources (MeReC) Bulletins. It also provides a tutorial about PACT (prescribing analysis and cost tabulation) data. PACT data are used to monitor and control prescribing cost, and are utilised at an individual practitioner level for ongoing education and clinical audit purposes.

The aim of the Patient Group Directions[48] site is to 'provide a centrally maintained archive of approved group protocols for the supply and administration of medicines'. Each patient group direction (PGD) is approved for use in a specific locality. The reason for publishing them in this way is to encourage other health professionals to evaluate them critically when they are considering producing their own protocols.

Druginfozone[49] is published in association with the London, South-East and Eastern Medicines Information Service. It publishes *Primary Care Journal Watch,* and has news and drug review features and links to the Medicines Information Services that produce the site.

One site that is dedicated to the crucial issue of why a high proportion of patients refuse or are unable to take the medication that is prescribed for them is the Concordance site.[50] This website has been developed by the Royal Pharmaceutical Society of Great Britain.

Patient information and patient advocacy

One of the most interesting changes brought about by the World Wide Web is the extraordinary range and variety of patient information sites. There is great concern that information on the Web is often too incomplete, inconsistent and erroneous to support decision making.

Nevertheless, people are increasingly turning to the Internet for information, and it is a serious challenge to provide them with the right type of information in the right format. Consider the case of NHS Direct Online,[51] the Web-based version of the NHS dial-up information service. It provides information directed at patients on numerous conditions. The information can be delivered in different languages, and audio files are available for all of them.

Dipex[52] – the Database of Individual Patient Experience – will be a site consisting of personal testimonies from patients suffering from diseases. The testimonies will be in the form of video, voice recordings or written accounts. At the moment the only conditions featured are hypertension and prostate cancer, but in time the site will expand to cover over 3000 major conditions.

The site is supported by the Department of Health and developed by the Department of Public and Primary Care at Oxford University in association with a coalition of patient advocate groups. One of the prime uses of the site will be as a means of educating medical staff about the key concerns of patients.

Patient UK[53] provides a considerable resource on common conditions. The Well Close Square Surgery site, as previously mentioned, has an archive of Patient Information Leaflets (PILs).

Designed to Involve[54] is an initiative set up in Scotland with the aim of giving primary care teams the opportunity to listen and act on the views of the public when planning services. The site features patient involvement methodologies and links to a range of patient advocate groups. One group that has a broad remit within primary care is the National Association for Patient Participation.[55]

Quality improvement

The National Primary Care Development Team was launched in February 2000, and was established to run the Primary Care Collaborative (PCC).[56] The site is intended to be a resource for those engaged in the work of the PCC, but more importantly it is of interest to anyone involved in quality improvement in primary care. The site has gathered together various documents and articles into collections headed 'spread of good practice'. Here you will find articles about access, capacity and demand management, the basics of clinical audit (Plan Do Study Act cycles) and quality improvement in coronary heart disease.

Some of the regional NHS modernising programmes are publishing details of schemes and initiatives for implementing NHS priorities. For example, Northern and Yorkshire Region[57] has published information about its primary care strategy.

The Clinical Practice Evaluation Programme (CPEP)[58] from the Royal College of General Practitioners (RCGP) is a quality improvement programme designed for a number of clinical conditions (coronary heart disease, adult asthma, type 2 diabetes foot care and adult depression). It forms part of the RCGP's Effective Clinical Practice Programme based at the School of Health and Related Research at the University of Sheffield (ScHARR).

The Clinical Governance Research and Development Unit (CGRDU)[59] at the University of Leicester is primarily concerned with the development of strategies for quality improvement in primary care. The site contains a number of audit templates developed by the CGRDU.

Local websites, often built around networks of primary care groups/primary care trusts, are flourishing. Some of these offer considerable resources in terms of sharing details of clinical audits and other clinical governance initiatives. Two of them are Equip,[60] 'an organisation responsible for the education of general practitioners in North Essex and their staff', and Suffolk Primary Care Resource Centre.[61]

Bandolier's[9] sister publication, ImpAct, covers quality improvement initiatives in primary care, and is a much-needed source of experience and expertise from real-life efforts.

Primary care groups and trusts will identify their own local health priorities, but these will often be based on Health Improvement Programmes (HImPs)[62] developed by health authorities. Many HImPs are available on the Web, although there is no single gateway collating them all.

The *Our Healthier Nation*[63] (OHN) website discusses the origin, criteria, content and processes of HImPs. This site contains a comprehensive collection of health promotion projects on the OHN in Practice database, which is searchable by health keyword (e.g. heart disease and stroke), target audience (e.g. carers, black and minority ethnic groups), Government initiative or zone associated with the project (e.g. Better Government for Older People Programme) and setting (e.g. GP surgery, home, healthy living centre, etc.).

Box 7.5 The Wisdom Centre

The Wisdom Centre delivers what it calls 'networked professional development' for primary care.[64]

The site is designed to help to develop personal learning plans and portfolios of evidence. The learning resources come in a number of formats ranging from documents written by the site developers themselves to seminars, distance learning materials and complete courses.

It pursues five main themes, namely health informatics, evidence-based practice, primary care group organisation, change management and clinical governance and quality assurance. The site hosts discussion groups around these themes, and encourages a dynamic relationship with its audience.

The Wisdom Centre site is innovative and forward thinking, using virtual conferences to test current themes and users' learning needs. It requires registration, but is free of charge.

References

1 http://www.nhs.uk/nhsplan/

Secondary sources of evidence

Evidence-based clinical practice guidelines

2 http://www.nice.org.uk/

3 http://www.sign.ac.uk/

4   http://www.eguidelines.co.uk
5   http://www.healthnet.org.uk/

Systematic reviews and critically appraised topics

6   http://www.update-software.com/clibhome/clib.htm
7   http://www.york.ac.uk/inst/crd/
8   http://www.nelh-pc.nhs.uk/
9   http://www.jr2.ox.ac.uk/bandolier/
10   http://cebm.jr2.ox.ac.uk/
11   http://www.york.ac.uk/inst/crd/em.htm
12   http://www.hda-online.org.uk/
13   http://www.hebs.scot.nhs.uk/

Protocols

14   http://www.wellclosesquare.co.uk/

Primary sources

15   http://194.66.253/ePrimaryCare/html/primary_main.html
16   http://www.innovate.org.uk
17   http://www.ucl.ac.uk/primcare-popsci/uebpp/uebpp.htm
18   http://www.update-software.com/nrr/CLIBINET.EXE?A=1&U=
     1001&P=10001
19   http://www.npcrdc.man.ac.uk/
20   http://www.kingsfund.org.uk/ePrimaryCare/html/national_evaluation_
     of_pcg.html
21   http://www.gpas.co.uk/
22   http://www.primary-care-db.org.uk/home.html

Tacit knowledge

23   http://www.jiscmail.ac.uk/lists/gp-uk.html
24   http://www.jiscmail.ac.uk/lists/HEALTH PROMOTION.html

25 http://www.jiscmail.ac.uk/PRIMSTAT.html

26 http://www.jiscmail.ac.uk/HAZ-EVALUATION.html

27 http://www.jiscmail.ac.uk/NETLIST.html

Policy in the four countries

28 http://www.doh.gov.uk/pricare/index.htm

29 http://www.show.scot.nhs.uk/

30 http://www.show.scot.nhs.uk/isd/

31 http://www.show.scot.nhs.uk/nhsstaff/header.htm

32 http://www.clinicalstandards.org/primcare.html

33 http://www.designedtoinvolve.org.uk

34 http://www.wales-nhs.uk/

35 http://www.primarycare-wales.org.uk/

Gateways

36 http://www.primarycarereport.co.uk/

37 http://www.ukpractice.net/ukpractice/aboutus/

38 http://www.synigence.net/healthcare/clinnixpro.htm

39 http://www.primarycare.co.uk/

40 http://www.nhsalliance.org/

41 http://www.primhe.org/

42 http://www.minorillness.co.uk/

Prescribing online

43 NHS Executive (1998) *GP Prescribing Support: a resource document and guide for the new NHS*. NHS Executive, Leeds. http://www.doh.gov.uk/nhsexec/gppres.htm

44 Brown H (2001) *View From the Frontline: online prescribing. He@lth Information on the Internet*. No 20 April 2001. Royal Society of Medicine Press Ltd, London; http://www.hioti.org

45 http://bnf.org

46 http://www.emims.net/

47 http://www.npc.co.uk/

48   http://www.groupprotocols.org.uk/
49   http://www.druginfozone.org/
50   http://www.concordance.org/

Patient information and patient advocacy

51   http://www.nhsdirect.nhs.uk/main.html
52   http://www.dipex.org/
53   http://www.patient.co.uk/
54   http://www.designedtoinvolve.org.uk/
55   http://www.napp.org.uk/

Quality improvement

56   http://www.npdt.org/
57   http://www.nyx.org.uk/modernprogrammes/primarycare/primary.html
58   http://www.shef.ac.uk/~scharr/publich/cpep/projsum.html
59   http://www.le.ac.uk/cgrdu/
60   http://www.equip.ac.uk/
61   http://www.suffolk-maag.ac.uk/
62   http://www.doh.gov.uk/nhsexec/briefnot/2798.htm
63   http://www.ohn.gov.uk/
64   http://www.wisdomnet.co.uk/

8

Coming to a screen near you

The Internet is the latest and most dramatic addition to what Stewart and Cohen call 'extelligence' – that is, the cumulative 'cultural capital' that lies all around us as books, videotapes, folk tales, and so on.[1] A society that fails to utilise extelligence risks relegation from the knowledge-driven economies to the ranks of the 'knowledge poor'. Knowledge generation, representation and application are powerful forces driving modern economic growth. Not surprisingly, governments are keenly interested in learning how to harness these forces, and are busily organising extelligence space.

So far in this book we have looked at how living in an Information Age is changing our lives in varied and subtle ways. We have identified the burdens and benefits characteristic of the Information Age, and we have considered how we must look for coping strategies and novel approaches to knowledge management if we are going to make the most of the opportunities for lifelong learning.

This final chapter takes a closer look at developments in extelligence space in the UK, with particular emphasis on health and other aspects of the public sector. In its report entitled *2020 Vision*,[2] the Library and Information Commission identified three priority areas to be tackled before the full potential of electronic delivery can be achieved, namely competencies, connectivity and content. We shall begin with the attempt to improve informatics skills among healthcare workers.

The three Cs: competencies, connectivity and content

The present Labour Government is perhaps the first that has been compelled to deal with acute Information Age issues. It quickly developed a wide-ranging information strategy and focused on 'transforming education, widening access, promoting competition and competitiveness, fostering quality and modernising government'. [3]

Health is a key target. The Government has pushed ahead with ambitious schemes to put in place 'the people, resources, culture and processes necessary to ensure that NHS clinicians and managers have the information needed to support the core purpose of the NHS in caring for individuals and improving public health'. [4]

Competencies

When the Labour Government was elected in 1997, there had been no consistent strategy tackling information management and technology skills across all professional groups at every level within the NHS. A plan to address skill deficits as part of a much wider strategy of renewal and reform was put in place with the national information strategy, *Information for Health: an information strategy for the modern NHS 1998–2005.*[5]

The targets set by *Information for Health* were updated by *Building the Information Core: implementing the NHS Plan.* [6] A sea change will be needed before the vision of a 'networked NHS' becomes a reality. The issues are clearly not just about resources for hardware and software: 'Everyone – individuals, multidisciplinary teams and care organisations – will need to think through the way that they work. Information is central to the process of redesigning care systems centred on the individual. Ensuring the quality of care involves being able to identify areas of weakness for individuals and teams, and to access and complete appropriate learning programmes'.[6]

The NHS Information Authority was one of the bodies charged with implementing *Information for Health* and developing core competency profiles for health informatics. The term 'health informatics' was defined in *Information for Health* as 'the effective use of information management and information and communications technology or recording and sharing information, and decision making to improve the planning and delivery of healthcare'.[5]

The Ways of Working with Information (WOWWI) section of the NHS IA published health informatics competencies in February 2001[2] (*see* Box 8.1). Although hardly revolutionary in themselves, they represent a crucial step towards bringing the NHS in line with Information Age developments.

Box 8.1 Health informatics competencies and the work of the NHS Information Authority

Health Informatics Competency Profiles for the NHS is the title of a critical document in the history of the NHS. The NHS IA details, for the first time, learning expectations and requisite skill levels for a spectrum of NHS staff.

Health informatics topics
The topics are grouped under the following headings:

- basic computing (personal computers, peripheral equipment, file management, networked facilities)
- basic applications (word processing, spreadsheets, databases, presentations, electronic mail, Internet browsing, time management)
- computer systems (clinical systems, non-clinical systems, management systems)
- data quality (data collection, data coding, data analysis, data audit, data standards)
- information management (identifying information needs, obtaining information, evaluating information, interpretation, decision making, communicating results)
- system development and strategic development
- clinical informatics (clinical record keeping, clinical decision support, clinical communications, clinical audit and evidence-based practice)
- communications technologies
- security and confidentiality (legislation, local policies and protocols, security mechanisms and standards)
- knowledge management (information searches, databases and library services, patient/public information, national infrastructure, case studies and research)
- health informatics skills (reviewing health informatics skills, user support, health informatics education, training and development).

Competency levels
Competency levels are ranked according to a five-point scale:

- 0: none – no knowledge or skills required
- 1: basic – a basic awareness and few, if any, skills required
- 2: intermediate – moderate skills and knowledge required
- 3: advanced – specialist skills and knowledge required
- 4: expert – full skills and knowledge required.

NHS staff groups
The document then links each subtopic of the health informatics areas to a competency level for each group of NHS staff. For example, registered nurses, midwives and health visitors are expected to have intermediate skills in basic computing and basic applications – with the exception of electronic mail, where advanced skills are required. However, this group of staff is expected to have advanced information management skills.

One of the key first steps is to increase skills in the fundamental informatics areas. The European Computer Driving Licence[7] (ECDL) will facilitate the training of NHS staff in basic computing and basic applications (*see* Box 8.2), and will be rolled out across the whole of the NHS.

Box 8.2 European Computer Driving Licence

As early as 1986, the Finnish Computer Society developed a series of modules for basic information technology skills. The European Computer Driving Licence (ECDL) was adopted in Finland as the national standard for IT competency, and was then taken up by other European Union member states. In 1996, the British Computer Society[8] took up the ECDL and promoted it within the UK. One million students have achieved the award since its inception.

The ECDL is now being used as the minimum standard within the NHS. The curriculum is designed to give anyone confidence in seven core skills:

1 basic concepts of IT
2 using a computer and managing files
3 word processing
4 spreadsheets
5 databases
6 presentations
7 information and communication.

NHS staff will have three years to complete the award, but preliminary studies have shown that most will complete the course in one year. The course is flexible so that staff moving from one trust to another around the country can add to the modules which they have successfully completed within the allocated timescale. The aim of the NHS Information Authority is to have most NHS employees holding the ECDL by 2005.

The competencies create a framework for the development of information management and technology skills within a modernised NHS. The NHS IA has already undertaken studies using the competency profiles to ascertain deficits as perceived by healthcare professionals themselves.[9] Annual surveys are planned until 2005. The results show how much work needs to be done before we have a workforce that is comfortable using basic information technology and routine information management tasks. The summary of the 2001 survey notes gloomily that only general medical practitioners and dental practitioners and career-grade hospital medical staff reached the recommended levels of competency in any of the designated topics, and that was in their basic knowledge of security mechanisms. Most other clinical staff (around half a million NHS staff) do not meet the recommended levels of competency in 'any of the topics'.

Connectivity

Wide variations in digital skills around the health service have not dampened efforts to create popular NHS-branded Internet sites, as the NHS Intranet[10] and My Workplace[11] projects testify (*see* Box 8.3). At this early stage in the evolution of the Internet, it seems reasonable to build structures and associated tools that are designed to be attractive to a large and diverse target group. Early adoption of My Workplace could accelerate the development of a true NHS virtual community exchanging all kinds of information, from jobs to clinical guidelines.

Box 8.3 NHS Intranet, My Workplace and zetoc via NeLH

NHS Intranet
The NHS Intranet is a joint venture between the NHS and BT Syntegra. The site is a gateway consisting of the following four 'channels':

- NHS today – 'daily news for people who work in healthcare'
- working – 'job-related information for people who work in healthcare'
- learning – 'learning resources for people who work in healthcare'
- living – 'lifestyle features and offers for people who work in healthcare'.

Although the site contains a 'learning' channel, the main early benefit for NHS employees will probably lie in the 'working' section. This covers pension information, such as retirement options, and pay scales linked to job descriptions and advice on careers. One of the most ambitious features will be an e-recruitment facility covering nationwide classifieds.

My Workplace
My Workplace offers NHS staff their own email address and operates in a similar manner to software such as Microsoft Outlook. Users can bookmark sites of interest and track their own learning needs through a scheduler. My Workplace will foster 'forums' on particular themes and push information to users via such recommended websites as the gateway for evaluated online resources for nursing, midwifery and allied health (NMAP).[12]

Knowledge-alerting service
NHS staff will also be able to access zetoc,[13] a British Library service, via the National electronic Library for Health. Zetoc gives access to the British Library of Electronic Table of Contents (ETOC) database, which is a research resource consisting of 16 million journal articles and conference papers that is updated daily. Users can set up alerts for journals of their choice. Whenever a new issue of a journal is published, the table of contents database is updated and this is emailed to users who have requested that journal's table of contents alert. NHS staff can use it to keep abreast of developments within their own field or fields of interest.

Despite having some good exemplar sites, NHS extelligence space still feels fragmented and discontinuous. It is inhabited by disparate sites and, with a few notable exceptions, there appears to have been no attempt to organise, structure or develop thematic ideas that would support health-care workers who are beginning to explore the medium.

A closely related term to connectivity is 'interoperability', which Paul Miller defines as a state of being 'actively engaged in the ongoing process of ensuring that the systems, procedures and culture of an organisation are managed in such a way as to maximise opportunities for exchange and reuse of information, whether internally or externally'.[14] He itemises the different flavours of interoperability, including technical and legal aspects. Progress is being made with the development of technical solutions for interconnectivity problems, and these will greatly enhance communications and data transfer across a range of media.

However, political and human interoperability is often overlooked, although it is just as important. Organisations that are absorbed with the technical challenges of system development often ignore or under-appreciate the implications for staff training, with obvious consequences for uptake and long-term use.

Inter-community interoperability is another challenge. Information seeking is routinely carried out across disciplines, yet users' ability to move between information-providing communities is often restricted. The barriers are a legacy of the type of institutionalised thinking that equated information giving with loss of control and ownership. Frustrated users might be forgiven for thinking that these barriers are an anachronism in an Information Age where traditional boundaries are rapidly dissolving.

Fortunately, a considerable number of initiatives exist across Government, education and public sectors where collaborations are working to help rather than to restrain interdisciplinary working. The projects listed below come from higher education, national and local government, public libraries and museums. The healthcare sector should learn from the creativity of the solutions that are offered here.

Box 8.4 Sharing information: e-Government, education, libraries, museums and archives

e-Government
The e-government strategy[15] concerns the use of technology to change the way in which Government at all levels is conducted. It addresses central government departments and their agencies, local government and the wider public sector, such as the National Health Service. A test site, the UK online Citizen Portal,[16] will provide 24-hour access to Government online information and services. Monthly reports from

the e-Minister and e-Envoy provide updates on implementation.[17] One strand is about extending access to electronic services, including the take-up of broadband services[18] (an Internet connection that is capable of handling large files, including video, in a fraction of the time currently experienced by most users). Statistics on the penetration of these technologies (e.g. the number of PCs per 100 pupils in primary/secondary education and the percentage of digital televisions among G8 countries) are available from the e-Stat Map at the Office of the e-Envoy.[19] The Digital Scotland Task Force is a similar initiative in Scotland.[20]

Interoperability issues are the focus of the e-Government Interoperability Framework (e-GIF).[21] Technical standards will be implemented to cope with the flow of information from different departments as well as the public sector. The Office of the e-Envoy will also undertake research to gain insight into the drivers and barriers to Internet use.

Libraries, museums and archives
The People's Network is the name given to the project to develop the UK Public Library Network.[22] This network will be the vehicle for providing access and support for the spread of information technology skills. The network will play a key role in lifelong learning projects and the University for Industry, and in supporting anyone who is undertaking self-development. One feature of the online presence of the People's Network is NETbase,[23] a database that tracks information developments in public libraries. It will include museums and archives information, as well as a directory of UK library Internet access points. Virtual museums will increase the number and variety of learning opportunities that are available.[24]

Education: higher and further education
The Joint Information Systems Committee (JISC)[25] is a strategic body that works on behalf of higher and further education in the UK. It funds dozens of projects aimed at bringing quality educational material online. These range from digitising museum collections to organising access to research material via a range of gateways. The gateways now cover an impressive range of disciplines, including the following:

• biosciences – BIOME[26]
• engineering, mathematics and computing – EEVL[27]
• humanities – HUMBUL[28]
• physical sciences – PSIgate[29]
• social sciences, business and law – SOSIG.[30]

Content

Connectivity is crucial to the rapid spread of knowledge. Without it, the NHS cannot begin to modernise itself in the ways that are envisaged by the NHS plan. Competencies are equally important, as without them the Government cannot review the development of essential skills in the workforce. However, without a rich and evolving content, staff will remain at the level of basic intelligence gathering when the true goal is real-world problem solving, expanding on the skills acquired through questioning, and searching.

As the online environment becomes richer and more diverse, so the learning opportunities increase. The number of potential teaching channels is also multiplying. The list of media available for electronic learning includes the Internet, intranets, video- and audio-conferencing, digital television, CD-ROM and DVD. Instruction can be shared between many users on a network, or through stand-alone personal computers.

Support for e-learning appears to be growing among both employers and employees (*see* Box 8.5).[31] For example, NHS staff taking the ECDL have benefited from both face-to-face teaching (c-learning) and e-learning. NHS Tayside has piped IT training materials to the desktops of more than 14 000 members of their staff.[32] Many suppliers are now offering similar courses on CD, but these can also be used over an intranet, Internet or similar network.

Box 8.5 Attitudes to e-learning: a national survey in 2000

The Campaign for Learning, KPMG, University for Industry and Peter Honey Learning undertook a joint survey of individual e-learners, employer budget holders for e-learning and providers of e-learning. It is probably the first survey of its kind in the UK.

Informal e-learning using the Internet was universal among the sample, although a high proportion of individuals had also been involved in some form of formal e-learning during the previous year. A significant number favoured CD-ROMs as a method of learning.

e-learners clearly felt in need of support, but 37% of employers did not offer any support for this type of training. Only 27% of organisations had dedicated PCs for learning, although most had the infrastructure to deliver e-learning materials. The majority of employers in the study spent less than 5% of their budget on e-learning.

Most e-learners felt positive about their learning experience, although there were mixed views. The main benefits were felt to be helping people to keep up to date, and they did not feel that the technology was a barrier to learning. Although the majority of trainers and employers felt that e-learning would greatly enhance their capacity to learn, nearly a quarter of the employers sampled were undecided about its potential. Neither employers nor trainers felt that the future lay entirely with e-learning, and they were divided about its cost-effectiveness. Training providers and employers recognised the potential of e-learning to tailor material to individual need, but few individuals associated this benefit with e-learning.

Individuals felt that the worst aspects of e-learning were its impersonal nature, and the loneliness and frustration due to lack of support. They felt that it was easy to waste time or experience some form of system failure. Both providers of e-learning material and employers feel that the medium is not sufficiently developed. The products can be too difficult to find, too gimmicky or of poor quality generally. Start-up costs were also considered to be prohibitive.

Myths of e-learning

e-learning certainly works, but it is wise to be clear about its limitations. The delivery of the ECDL via electronic means makes economic sense, as the medium is so efficient at disseminating information to large numbers of people and over a large geographical area. But is it the panacea that the NHS is looking for and will it suit all topics? Reports from the USA suggest that despite the sophistication of technology, the computer will not replace the classroom for several reasons (see Table 8.1).[33]

Communities of practice

Whatever the blend of electronic facilitated or conventional learning, it is important that healthcare staff are engaged and supported in whatever style of learning they choose. Most individuals in the e-learning survey were happy with informal e-learning for either basic awareness or knowledge upkeep. However, the real dividends will come when those same individuals grow more comfortable with the medium and begin to exploit its potential for collaborative projects and team learning. Then the medium will be put at the service of real-world problem solving.

Table 8.1 Limitations of e-learning
(adapted from *The Myth and Realities of e-Learning* by Don Clark)

The hype	*The reality*
Always 'on', 24-hour access	Only true if you have a connection and technology that can cope with the downloading and delivery of the e-learning material. Even where this is true, a desktop in a ward or office is not conducive to learning
Richness of content through use of multimedia – audio, video, access to discussion groups, etc.	Depends on how much bandwidth is available. Conventional learning can match some of these features
Can be tailored to suit an individual's learning style (e.g. self-paced)	There is no automatic accounting for learning style
Ability to link to other resources (other content, study groups, etc.). No need to be bound by the linearity of book learning	Conventional study programmes can offer this, too
The learner is not the passive recipient of material, but a self-directed, proactive intelligence gatherer	Often e-learning programmes are nothing more than repackaged conventional learning with little effort to make use of this feature
e-learning materials are modular in design	But so is conventional learning
The effectiveness of e-learning programmes can be easily measured	The number of downloads is not an adequate measure of effectiveness. Traffic across a site does not tell the whole story. Most usability research points to the need for qualitative analysis and direct observation to supplement these figures
Cannot be beaten for delivering cost-effective model for education	Depends on uptake, suitability of material for target audience, technical infrastructure, support, etc.
Storage capacity – the Internet or learning network provides a capacity far beyond the learner's hard drive or physical classroom environment	Again, so much depends on factors such as bandwidth and the quality of courseware

One of the most difficult aspects for e-learning to replicate is the social aspect of learning in groups. Group learning challenges an individual's own beliefs by exposure to different viewpoints, experiences and solutions. Not every group develops this type of dynamic, but those that do can be called communities of practice.[34] Communities of practice share the following characteristics.

- They form out of social or professional ties.
- They habitually use each other as sounding boards and actively collaborate with each other.
- They tend to come together through a common aim.
- They cannot be created artificially. Groups form and fall apart quickly.
- They develop customs and a culture of their own.
- They are independent by nature.
- They are critical to the organisation's learning and development.

Ideally, communities of practice will seize the networking opportunities offered by the Internet while continuing to benefit from the type of fusion of ideas that is only available through face-to-face learning. The access to diverse resources from a range of disciplines should encourage the type of 'open systems thinking' that is intrinsic to a learning organisation such as the modernised NHS (*see* Box 8.6).

Box 8.6 Developing learning organisations

The modernisation of the NHS is predicated on it truly becoming an organisation that learns, acknowledges mistakes, develops a deeper understanding of why these occur, shares innovations and implements solutions. What are the other features of the learning organisation? Davies and Nutley[35] have summarised recent theories about how organisations learn and applied it to the health service.

Learning takes place at several levels. Single loop learning consists of diagnosing problems and undertaking remedial, incremental action to improve practice. In double loop learning, systems are reviewed and goals and priorities are reassessed. Triple loop learning occurs when lessons learned from that experience are translated across departments or other care processes.

Open systems thinking. The disease model shapes many of the structures and services throughout the health service. It promotes the expert but perpetuates isolationism and disconnectedness. Open systems thinking encourages reintegration and looks outside these internal structures and the boundaries around the organisation.

Team learning and improving individual capabilities. The organisation will encourage self-development, but not at the expense of group learning, since healthcare is delivered not by virtuosi but by competent individuals working in teams.

Updating mental models. These are the deep-seated assumptions that shape the way in which individuals see the world and constrain what they see as possible within the organisation. Challenging these mental models will be essential to finding new ways of working.

Sharing knowledge

Knowledge management and e-learning are closely related. Knowledge management in a modernised NHS means capturing the knowledge of its staff and employing e-learning as part of its tactics to develop team collaborations, individual capabilities and other features of learning organisations.

The performance of the NHS is under severe scrutiny. Reports describing it as a 'passive' as opposed to 'active' learning organisation have followed investigations into catastrophic failures.[36,37] However, many organisations struggle with knowledge management, and the vast reservoir of workforce knowledge remains impervious to their efforts to harness it. Real group learning collaborations – communities of practice – are difficult to create, but a learning organisation will find ways to foster them.

One of the key activities of knowledge management is the transformation of tacit knowledge into explicit knowledge. Tacit knowledge is the type that Charles Leadbeater describes as 'acquired by doing and transmitted by example'.[38] It is 'often learned by osmosis, over long periods, in very particular contexts'. Books, articles, reports and the Internet exemplify explicit knowledge – the stuff of extelligence space. The key is that explicit knowledge is transferable, even though some of the richness of learning by example can be lost in translation.

Knowledge transmitted by example is slow and inefficient, although it can produce exceptional results. The craft skills of traditional industries were spread in this way. This is not an argument for more waves of information, but rather for looking at ways in which intelligence and extelligence can interact more productively. e-learning could greatly facilitate this process.

Leadbeater[38] uses cooking and recipe writing as a potent analogy of the knowledge economy. Recipes are an example of tacit knowledge that is transformed into explicit knowledge. There are many repercussions of this transfer of knowledge, some of which are obvious, while others are insidious but the effect of the impact is deep and long-lasting. Although the fixed costs of developing the recipe can be large, once a recipe has been perfected it costs little to reproduce it hundreds or thousands of times. It can be reformatted and disseminated through multiple channels (e.g. Delia Smith's recipes proliferate through television, books, magazines and newspaper supplements). The knowledge and expertise that went into creating the recipe are thus spread. The process is dynamic – as the recipe goes out into the world, users transform, amend and adapt it, and use and reuse it.

Users get increasingly drawn into the process as products become more knowledge intensive. The lessons from food economy do not end here. As the area grows increasingly knowledge intensive, so knowledge transmission becomes more efficient, choice increases and resources are used more creatively. The knowledge encapsulated in the recipe is not consumed – it does not perish, but rather it multiplies by transmission and increases the impact. 'We have made social and economic progress by replacing a relatively narrow, inefficient method of knowledge transmission with a far more effective range of mechanisms to spread know-how more widely, which is both more efficient and fun.'[38]

Recipes and their proxies, such as software programs, are extremely important to knowledge management and have a dramatic impact on the way in which we work. An important example from healthcare is the development of care pathways (*see* Box 8.7).

Box 8.7 Transformation of tacit knowledge into explicit knowledge: care pathways

Integrated care pathways define the expected timing and course of events in the care of a patient with a particular condition, and describe explicitly all of the expected processes of care.[39] Many trusts and NHS organisations are actively engaged in developing care pathways. However, there is no central resource to help them in this complex and onerous task.

In 1998, the Royal College of Nursing (RCN) undertook a survey of the NHS in order to ascertain the extent to which care pathways were being planned, piloted, implemented and evaluated. The survey was repeated in 2000/2001.

The development of the National electronic Library for Health (NeLH) provided the opportunity to examine how the data from the RCN survey might be shared with a much wider audience. Over 2000 records from the RCN database were transferred to a 'digital box' maintained by the NeLH. Details of care pathway co-ordinators and the care pathway topics can be searched, and actual care pathway documentation will be linked to records.

In time, further resources will be added to the site (e.g. appraisal checklists). Care pathway co-ordinators will be able to edit and update their own records.

The RCN survey showed that duplication of effort was endemic to care pathway development. The survey identified nearly 50 care pathways for total hip replacement alone. Now the NeLH has a unique resource that is accessible by thousands online, with the potential to feed into communities of practice engaged in real-life problem solving.[40]

Futurology

Let us imagine the not too distant future. The NHS university is fully functioning (*see* Box 8.8).[41] Thousands of staff regularly take part in a wide variety of courses, including NHS induction, and obligatory programmes on information management and technology and safety.

Box 8.8 The NHS university

During the run-up to the 2001 election, the Government announced plans for a 'flexible' university for the NHS. Statements suggest that the university, to be established by 2003, would be run as a partnership between the NHS, existing universities and the private sector.

Low-paid NHS staff would receive a sum of money for use in their 'learning account'. Courses would be tailored to suit the diverse groups that constitute the largest employer in Europe. The type of subject areas might include social care, nursing training, technology, mathematics, computing and management skills. An expected 100 000 NHS staff would join the NHS university.

The courses are delivered in a blend of e-learning and conventional learning. Team learning is a regular occurrence, and is mandatory for certain subjects, such as patient safety and quality improvement. Multi-professional teams are revalidated, not just individuals. Simulation tools for training purposes are widespread, especially for safety critical contexts.

Box 8.9 Safety and learning in the NHS

Let us imagine a scenario concerning patient safety in the NHS. It is no exaggeration to say that any judgement as to whether the NHS has the ability to become an 'active' learning organisation will depend on how this issue is tackled. The scenario looks at patient safety in terms of the issues discussed in this chapter – that is, competency, connectivity and content. It touches on fundamental issues of interoperability, sharing of knowledge and learning organisations. The National Patient Safety Agency (NPSA)[42] is the setting for this scenario. Some of the features described are already part of the site.

The NPSA is one of the most visited NHS sites. It organises content and provides structured access to an extensive knowledge base on safety-related issues, policy documents from the four countries, quality initiatives, primary research and patient-related sites. It monitors and hosts discussion boards and encourages the participation of staff from every quarter of the organisation, and also from outside it.

The National Reporting System for adverse health events submits scenarios to the site. These are organised in a searchable directory. The scenarios form the basis of regular root-cause analyses. These in turn are used as source material for the educational programme. The site makes available various tools to support group collaborations, such as heuristic reporting forms to facilitate local safety projects.

The NPSA site links to the educational agenda of the NHS university. Half of the hours spent in continuing education are to be devoted to patient safety education. Courses are available through the NHS university at several levels. Now that broadband technology is with us, many of the courses are broadcast as full video programmes with interactive components.[43] The 'intelligent' system underpinning the online learning environment logs each completed module and updates the user's learning record. As each lifelong learning student has registered his or her professional details, adverse event alerts can be passed to them.

A National Health Informatics Forum (NHIF)[44] has been established to set the public agenda for biomedical and health information. It brings together interests from a range of disciplines, including knowledge management and e-educationalists.

The NHIF invests in a massive multidisciplinary programme. Knowledge management tools will be a priority, but the research programme will take a wide-ranging approach to the health information needs of the public, patients, nurses, doctors and other staff.

No single entry point exists for evaluated websites. However, higher education-funded gateways are recognised for the reliability of their services, and continue to be supported by professional bodies whose members benefit from their existence. Cross-searching facilities exist between the gateways and the content of the National electronic Library for Health. Websites that record patient experiences flourish.

Information overload clinics begin to appear. These treat a range of stress-related Information Age conditions, including infonesia[45] (the inability to remember where one saw a piece of information) and internesia[45] (the inability to remember on which website one saw a piece of information). Internesiacs are often placed on harsh treatment regimes. These consist of abstention from email and the recommended use of rubber-mouse stress toys. The 'doctors' are qualified informatics experts who dispatch advice and words of wisdom on all aspects of knowledge management.

Conclusion

It is all too easy to get carried away with crystal-ball gazing. The Internet polarises views like no other development, leading us into cycles of hype followed by disappointment.

Certain driving forces, such as consumer experiences with Internet shopping and email, are shaping expectations about online health information. However, the barriers remain, namely concerns about security, the variability of online information and clinician scepticism.[46] The situation is made even more problematic by the state of legacy information systems and serious shortages of development funding and skilled personnel.

Yet there is room for guarded optimism. Responsibility and leadership are evident. The information environment is evolving and becoming a richer place for lifelong learning. We need to develop the requisite skills to be able to exploit it. Change in education practice is slow, but the ability to formulate search strategies and the ability to use knowledge representation tools are critical skills. The need to acquire them is made paramount by this Information Age. Professor Joseph Novak, champion of concept mapping, wrote that perhaps there may come a time when such methods will be commonplace: 'Hopefully, by the year 2061, this will come to pass.'[47]

Summary

- Electronic service delivery is transforming all areas of the public sector, including health.
- The Government's information policy is addressing three critical issues, namely competencies, connectivity and content.
- The NHS Information Authority has mapped out the main informatics areas for each group of health services workers, and has assigned expected levels of achievement for each area.
- The European Computer Driving Licence (ECDL) is now used throughout the NHS as a measure of competence in basic computing and computing applications.
- The NHS is introducing projects designed to personalise online access for NHS staff and increase uptake of electronic information services.
- Government, public libraries, museums and higher education are also developing effective electronic channels.
- Connectivity is closely allied to interoperability – not simply technological but also human factors and communications between disciplines are important.

- e-learning will play a prominent role in helping NHS staff with their lifelong learning needs. However, there are limitations to e-learning that need to be recognised.
- The NHS needs to invest in ways of accessing the deep, tacit knowledge of its employees and making it available in explicit forms, so that it can be used and reused throughout the service.
- Healthcare staff should be comfortable using electronic media such as the Internet for real-life problem solving if competencies, connectivity and content are managed successfully.
- There will be many opportunities for e-learning in the future. The challenge will be to use the increasing diversity of Web content to ensure that the experience is stimulating and fun.

References

1 Stewart I and Cohen J (1997) *Fragments of Reality*. Cambridge University Press, Cambridge.

2 Library and Information Commission (1998) *2020 Vision*. Library and Information Commission, London; http://www.lic.gov.uk/publications/policyreports/20202.html

3 Blair A (1998) *Our Information Age: the Government's vision*. Central Office of Information, London.

4 NHS Information Authority (2001) *Health Informatics Competency Profiles for the NHS*. NHS Information Authority, Winchester.

5 Department of Health (1998) *Information for Health: an information strategy for the modern NHS 1998–2005*. DoH, London.

6 Department of Health (2001) *Building the Information Core: implementing the NHS Plan*. DoH, London.

7 http://www.nhsia.nhs.uk/wowwi/ecdl

8 http://www.ecdl.co.uk/

9 NHS Information Authority (2001) *National Health Informatics Competency. Annual Survey*. NHS Information Authority, Winchester.

10 http://www.nhsintranet.nhs.uk/

11 http://www.nelh.nhs.uk/myworkplace

12 http://nmap.ac.uk/

13 http://www.bl.uk/services/zetoc/overview.html

14 Miller P (2001) *Interoperability: what is it and why should I want it?* http://www.ariadne.ac.uk/issue24/interoperability

15 Performance and Innovation Unit (2000) *e-gov: electronic government services for the twenty-first century*. Cabinet Office, London; http://www.cabinet-office.gov.uk/innovation/2000/delivery/e-gov.pdf

16 http://www.ukonline.gov.uk/

17 Office of the e-Envoy (2001) *UK Online: the broadband future*. Cabinet Office, London.

18 http://www.e-envoy.gov.uk/publications/reports/broadband/index.htm

19 http://www.e-envoy.gov.uk/estatmap/estatmap.htm

20 http://www.scotland.gov.uk/digitalscotland/

21 http://www.e-envoy.gov.uk/publications/frameworks/egif2/

22 http://www.ukoln.ac.uk/services/lic/newlibrary/

23 http://www.peoplesnetwork.gov.uk/netbase/index.html

24 http://www.lic.gov.uk/publications/policyreports/building/index.html

25 http://www.jisc.ac.uk/

26 http://www.biome.ac.uk/

27 http://www.eevl.ac.uk/

28 http://www.humbul.ac.uk/

29 http://www.psigate.ac.uk/

30 http://www.sosig.ac.uk/

31 http://www.educationalmultimedia.com

32 *Atttitudes to e-Learning: a national survey 2000*; http://www.campaign-for-learning.org.uk/news/elearning.htm

33 Clark D (2001) *Reflections on e-Learning*; http://www.nwlink.com/~donclark/hrd/elearning/intro.html

34 Seely Brown J (1991) *Organisational Learning and Communities of Practice*. Institute of Management Sciences, Rhode Island; http://www.parc.xerox.com/ops/members/brown/papers/orglearning.html. Further references for communities of practice can be found at http://www.teleport.com/~smithjd/CP_bibl/

35 Davies HTO and Nutley S (2000) Developing learning organisations in the new NHS. *BMJ*. **320**: 998–1001.

36 Expert Group on Learning from Adverse Events in the NHS (2000) *An Organisation With a Memory*. The Stationery Office, London; http://www.doh.gov.uk/orgmemreport/index.htm

37 Bristol Royal Infirmary Inquiry (2001) *Learning from Bristol: the report of the public inquiry into children's heart surgery at the Bristol Royal Infirmary 1984–1995*. The Stationery Office, London; http://www.bristol-inquiry.org.uk/

38 Leadbeater C (1999) *Living on Thin Air*. Penguin Books, Harmondsworth.

39 Kitchiner D and Bundred P (1996) Integrated care pathways. *Arch Dis Child.* **75**: 166–8.

40 http://www.nelh.nhs.uk/carepathways.asp

41 This prediction is one of the recommendations from the Government-led Foresight programme http://www.foresight.gov.uk/. It appears in *Health Care 2020*.

42 http://www.npsa.org.uk/

43 http://www.keep-up-to-date.tv

44 http://www.foresight.gov.uk/

45 http://www.whatis.techgtarget.com/

46 Mittman R and Cain M (1999) *The Future of the Internet in Health Care. Five-year forecast.* California Health Care Foundation, Oakland, CA; http://ehealth.chcf.org/

47 Novak JD (2000) *The Theory Underlying Concept Maps and How to Construct Them*; http://cmap.coginst.uwf.edu/info/printer.html

Index